ADVANCE PRAISE FOR

"The beauty of this book is that it is co. *... ... ... every man I counsel, to work through Pure at Heart."*

Kirk Durston, Director, New Scholars Society
Campus Crusade for Christ
Wallenstein, Ontario, Canada

"Sexual purity is one of the most difficult areas to discuss in family life but Dr. Sheh's book makes this subject accessible. His analysis and medical insights into pornography addiction gives us solid tools for freedom and healing. He helps us understand God's best for sexuality and gives a road map to get there – I highly recommend this book."

Lorna Dueck, Listen Up TV & Faith Commentary Writer
Burlington, Ontario, Canada

"In too many Christian books about sexual purity, a man's sexual wiring is too often demonized and vilified. Dr. Sheh, on the other hand, brings balance to this important topic. Along with that balance, he also brings some new strategies for dealing with sexual purity that is both psychologically and scripturally sound. I have no doubt that this material will make a significant impact on men struggling with this issue."

Geof Cornelson, Former Director of Clergy Care
Focus on the Family (Canada)
Langley, British Columbia, Canada

"Dr. Sheh asks some tough questions when it comes to men, pornography and sexual addiction – is it just about sex? The reasons behind these habits may surprise you, as may the practical plan to get free from these family and self-destroying habits. This book is a must read, both for men and women who are looking for answers."

Paul Arthur, TV Host
"IN SIGHT" Television Talk Show, the Miracle Channel
Lethbridge, Alberta, Canada

"Pure at Heart is a welcome handbook on pursuing sexual purity. Dr. Sheh combines biblical principles with medical and psychological insights to show the destructiveness of pornography while at the same time offering practical strategies for redirecting sexual energy in a healthy direction. Written in a brisk, 'point-form' style, the handbook is quick to read, but, if applied with God's help, can change your life for good!"

Dr. Ed Stuckey, Former Senior Pastor
Ellerslie Road Baptist Church
Edmonton, Alberta, Canada

PURE AT HEART

Revised & Expanded

A MAN'S GUIDE TO PURITY IN A SEXUALIZED WORLD

DR. SIMON SHEH

Simon Sheh & Associates

Dr. Simon Sheh

Pure at Heart: Revised & Expanded
A Man's Guide to Purity in a Sexualized World

Published by: Simon Sheh & Associates

#154 Meadowlark Health Centre
156 Street and 87 Avenue
Edmonton, Alberta
Canada T5R 5W9

DIGITALLY PRINTED BY

PageMaster
PUBLICATION SERVICES INC.

ISBN 978-1-897544-12-9
Printed in Canada

To Helen, Ian, and Naomi,
who constantly inspired me
to write and publish
Pure at Heart

FOREWORD

If you listen to the many voices of western culture, the primary pathway to happiness is through sexual permissiveness. The elusive pursuit of pleasure has trapped millions of men in sexual sin. The lure and ready access of pornography, the erosion of sexual mores has many Christian men living in defeat.

You'll soon learn that this author, as a counselor, has heard all the rationalizations that accompany sexual sin. He's listened to the heartache of those wanting release from destructive sexual attitudes and addictions.

Dr. Sheh points us to another pathway; one of freedom and victory. The word of God through the Holy Spirit is able to tear down strongholds of the imagination. The power of God can make possible what seems unchangeable.

The book is characterized by its practical, forthright insights into overcoming the temptations of sexual passion. It succinctly exposes the false reasoning of our hyper-sexualized world. Most importantly, it provides a clear pathway towards sexual purity.

I am glad to recommend this book to the Christian public.

Dr. Keith C. Taylor, Senior Pastor, Beulah Alliance Church
Edmonton, Alberta, Canada, March 2006

PREFACE

This book is the product of my Pure at Heart Seminar that I've conducted in churches in Canada since April 2003. The Pure at Heart Seminar is a one-day, biblically-based, teaching seminar that equips men to pursue purity in our hyper-sexualized world. There are two main reasons why I created the Pure at Heart Seminar and subsequently turned the seminar material into a book.

First, I have witnessed many times in my counseling practice the devastating impacts and consequences of addiction to pornography, inappropriate Internet relationships, and extra-marital affairs on a man's mental health, his marriage, family life, work, and ministry. Sexual addiction is treatable. Affairs outside of marriage are preventable. I want every man to have the right tools to be a champion of purity in his home, his work place, and public arenas. Men want tools, and this book is about practical tools that men can use in their life time to pursue purity.

Second, I struggled with pornography in my younger years and God has healed me and showed me healthy ways to take care of myself instead of running to pornography for self-medication. I believe the power of God's healing is available to every man in His kingdom.

My vision is every man pure at heart in the kingdom of God. My mission is to equip every man to pursue purity in our sexualized world.

Sexual purity is every man's battle. This book is not only written for men who struggle with pornography or inappropriate virtual-relationships on the Internet. This book is also designed for every man, every young adult and older teenager, every father, every pastor and clergy, every missionary, and every church and ministry leader who wants to answer the call from God to be a champion of purity in His kingdom.

This book presents an extremely honest examination of a man's life, his mind, and his conduct. If the messages in this book clearly speak to you and convict your heart, I strongly encourage you to seek wise counsel without delay so that you can experience healing and restore healthy and godly living. God bless.

Dr. Simon Sheh
Edmonton, Alberta
Canada
June 2006

CONTENTS

Chapter One
THE CALL TO BE GODLY — 1

Chapter Two
KNOWING YOURSELF — 7

Chapter Three
KNOWING YOUR ENEMY — 27

Chapter Four
LIFE TIME PURE AT HEART TOOLS FOR HEALTHY
AND GODLY LIVING — 35

Chapter Five
BRAIN ECONOMICS AND PORNOGRAPHY
ADDICTION — 55

Chapter Six
SHAME AND PORNOGRAPHY ADDICTION — 59

Chapter Seven
RE-CLAIM YOUR PATHWAY TO GODLINESS — 66

Chapter Eight
AFFAIR-PROOF YOUR MARRIAGE — 72

Chapter Nine
CREATING A LEGACY OF PURITY IN THE FAMILY — 82

Chapter Ten
STAY EQUIPPED IN YOUR JOURNEY — 87

Recommended Reading — 91
About the Pure at Heart Seminar — 94
About the Author — 96
Acknowledgements — 97
Book order information — 98

CHAPTER ONE

THE CALL TO
BE GODLY

"We are called, like Christ, to be godly, but we are expected to live it out fully in the midst of others. There is no more dangerous path than the one trodden by Jesus."

From Michael Frost's *Exiles: Living Missionally in a Post-Christian Culture*

In the world of business and human resource management, people are not the most important asset. The right people are. In the world of God's kingdom, Christian men are not the most important asset. Godly men are.

God did not first call us the name Christians. It was in Antioch, recorded in the book of Acts, chapter 11:26, "and in Antioch the disciples were first called Christians." The title began as a nickname. The people of Antioch, who were pagans, were famous for their ability to create mocking nicknames. Christian means these Christ-folk. It began as a contemptuous nickname; but the Christians took it and made it known to the entire world. By their lives they made "Christian" a name of respect, admiration and even wonder.

A name is very important, especially for men and women who run a business and for people who excel in sales and marketing. We have heard of brand names and designer names. In Canadian politics, the name "Liberal" is not a very popular name in Western Canada. My wife is a nurse who works in a local hospital. One day she said, "If I am sick, please don't let Dr. ABC (not the real name) treat me." I guess Dr. ABC does not have a good name among the nurses in the hospital. You might hear from your high school kid, "Please don't give me Mr. XYZ (not the real name) for my Math 30 please." Mr. XYZ must not enjoy a good name among the students. A good name means a lot.

It is not the name that attracts attention - it is what is behind the name. In business, there are five value attributes that make a business a successful enterprise. They are: price, accessibility, products, service, and experience. Price and experience have made the name West Jet a successful discount airline in Western Canada. Quality products and good customer service have provided the name Eddie Bauer its loyal followers in Canada and the U.S.

What was behind the name Christian that attracted the Antioch pagans? I believe it is godliness that was manifested in the lives of Christ's followers. I believe God calls you and me to be godly - to be godly men. The name or the word "Christian" is only mentioned three times in the entire Bible: Acts 11:26, Acts 26:28, and 1Peter 4:16. But the words godly and godliness are cited in the Bible 30 times. First and 2Timothy and Titus are the three most personal letters that the apostle Paul wrote. He wrote not to a congregation, but to two young men, Timothy and Titus, who were in ministry. These three letters are called the "pastoral epistles." They are highly personal, practical, and unsystematic in nature. They are also among the last words Paul wrote, and they reflected the sort of concerns that burdened the apostle near the end of his ministry.

In these three letters alone, the word godliness is mentioned ten times (1Tim 2:2, 3:16, 4:7-8, 6:3, 5-6, 11; 2Tim 3:5; Titus 1:1). Consider godliness is mentioned 30 times in the Bible, and in these three personal letters alone, Paul mentioned godliness ten times. Paul wrote these very personal letters at the end of his ministry. Godliness must have been his burden, and it was something he wanted Timothy and Titus and all Christian men and women to pursue. In 1Timonthy 6:6, the apostle wrote, "and it is, indeed, a source of immense profit, for godliness accompanied with contentment is great and abundant gain" (The Amplified Bible). Then, in verse 11, Paul addressed Timothy as man of God and instructed him to pursue righteousness, godliness, faith, love, patience, and gentleness. Godliness was in Paul's heart. If Apostle Paul wanted to write you and me a personal letter today, it would be his passion that you and I pursue godliness. The apostle understood that godliness is the core value attribute for Christians to attract people to their lives.

WHAT IS GODLINESS?

I believe one of the core value attributes behind godliness is blamelessness. God does not call us to be perfect; He calls us to be blameless. Blamelessness is one of the themes in the passage for church leaders described in 1Timothy 3: Leaders must be above reproach, have a good reputation and be well thought of by those outside the church. Leaders must also acquire a good standing for themselves. I want you to realize God does not demand any less from you and me. Even if we are not elders and deacons, we are leaders in our workplace, in the marketplace, in schools, and, most of all, we are leaders in our homes and marriages. God calls you and me to be godly, and He calls you and me to be blameless. Out of blamelessness comes a man of integrity, a man of honor.

Nowadays, the name Christian is somewhat overrated. Sam is a Christian teacher; therefore he must be an excellent teacher. Not necessarily. Joe is a Christian businessman; therefore he must be an honest businessman. Not necessarily. Bob is a manager, and he is a Christian; therefore he must be a good manager. Not necessarily.

The name Christian has lost its value and impact. In November 2003, country music singer Glen Campbell was arrested for "extreme drunken driving" after a collision in Phoenix, Arizona. According to the December 8, 2003 edition of Time Magazine, the evangelical Christian said he forgot that the anti-anxiety medication he was taking shouldn't be mixed with alcohol.

Christian and godliness are NOT synonymous. Christian is no guarantee for godliness. Religious positions (ministers, elders, deacons, Sunday school teachers, missionaries, etc.) and godliness are not synonymous either. A Christian man is not necessary a godly man. You and I need to take full responsibility for ourselves, because we have not been blameless in our thoughts and actions. We need to listen to the Apostle Paul. We need to pursue godliness, and practice blamelessness.

ARE YOU BLAMELESS?

- When you look at a woman in the public and in the church?
- When you relate to a woman who is not your wife?
- When you go online on the Internet?

- When you watch TV and DVDs?
- When you read a magazine at the news stand?

ARE YOU BLAMELESS IN
THE PURSUIT OF PURITY?

In God's kingdom, every man is called to be a champion of purity, both inwardly and outwardly. In the Bible, there are three key Biblical passages on purity:

"Blessed (happy, enviably fortunate, and spiritually prosperous – by the experience of God's favour and especially conditioned by the revelation of His grace, regardless of their outward conditions) are the pure in heart, for they shall see God!"

(Matthew 5:8, the Amplified Bible)

"Who shall go up into the mountain of the Lord? Or who shall stand in His Holy Place? He who has clean hands and a pure heart, who has not lifted himself up to falsehood or to what is false, nor sworn deceitfully. He shall receive blessing from the Lord and righteousness from the God of his salvation."

(Psalm 24:3-5, the Amplified Bible)

"Create in me a clean heart, O God, and renew a right, persevering, and steadfast spirit within me."

(Psalm 51:10, the Amplified Bible)

In God's kingdom, every man is called to live a life of purity. In the kingdom's business, this is a key character of a godly man. His whole life, public and private, is transparent before God, men, and women. His very heart - including his thoughts and motives – is free of deceit, dishonesty, and a double life.

The following is a true story of deceit, dishonesty, and a

double life published in the January 17, 2005 edition of the *Edmonton Journal*.

> *Katie, a middle-age Ontario woman, who commutes in a 2001 Volkswagen Jetta to panhandle for herself and her children outside the Eaton Centre in Toronto, Canada before driving home to an upscale, $333,000.00 house outside of Toronto, owned by her husband, says she's "just trying to get by." One of Katie's daughters is 25 and lives on her own.*

Dear men and brothers in Christ, let us once and for all shun leading double lives and commit ourselves to be godly men and champions of purity so that we can see God now with the eye of faith and see His glory in the hereafter.

LET THE WORK AND JOURNEY OF PURITY BEGIN!

CHAPTER TWO

KNOWING YOURSELF

"Many people don't know the difference between physical attraction or sexual arousal, and lust. They are not the same. God made every one of us a sexual being and that is good. Attraction and arousal are the natural, spontaneous, God-given response to physical beauty, while lust is a deliberate act of the will. Lust is a choice to commit in your mind what you'd like to do with your body. You can be attracted or even aroused without choosing to sin by lusting. Many people, especially Christian men, feel guilty that their God-given hormones are working. When they automatically notice an attractive woman, they assume it is lust and feel ashamed and condemned. But attraction is not lust until you begin to dwell on it."

From Rick Warren's *Purpose Driven Life*

We are made sexual beings by God. Sex within marriage is natural, not shameful. Life itself is borne of sex! Physical attraction to the opposite sex is natural and normal. Eve was the first Miss Universe, undoubtedly the most impeccable woman ever to walk on earth. When Adam first saw Eve, he was almost speechless. He said, "WOW MAN!" and he named her woman.

When a man purposefully looks at and focuses his attention on the sexual parts of a woman's body and nothing else, he treats the woman as a sexual object and uses her body to fulfill something missing in him. As a result, the man objectifies and sexualizes women, i.e., sees them as an assemblage of breasts, legs, and buttocks. In doing so, he risks forming a dependency on visual imagery for arousal. Men and women are all created with a body, a mind, and a spirit. When a man sexually objectifies a woman by focusing only on her body parts, it is a form of splitting up the creation of God and denying and disrespecting the value of the whole person. In essence, the man is subtly and indirectly abusing the woman.

In the Western world, we live in an increasingly hyper-sexualized world. *The National Post* of Canada reported on December 31, 2004 that in the United States, plastic surgeons admit the prediction of smaller breast implants on women is wishful thinking. With more women undergoing augmentation procedures and the average American implant size ranging from 400 to 600 ml – about the volume of a small bottle of water – the doctors say breasts cannot get any larger. Dr. Leroy Young, a St. Louis, Missouri plastic surgeon with the American Society for Aesthetic Plastic Surgery, blames the popularity of large implants on the influence of pornography on American mainstream culture. In California, there is a non-profit website where men finance breast enlargements for women around the world by donating what they like in return for innocent to explicit photos, videos and online chat. In England, Sarah-Kate Templeton of the *Sunday Times* reported on July 10, 2005 that British students are resorting to breast surgery before starting university because they fear they will otherwise lack the confidence to meet new friends and succeed in their studies. Some London surgeons report that several students a week turn to them in drastic attempts to boost their self-esteems. There are concerns that some British surgeons may be trading on the insecurities of young students who should be left free to develop their sense of identity without commercial pressures.

Interestingly, bigger breasts don't necessarily solve big problems. A Swedish study, reported in the October/November 2003 issue of *Healthy Women*, indicated that a woman may end up with big breasts but still have significant problems. The Swedish study revealed that women who undergo augmentations are three times more likely to commit suicide than women who are happy with their natural breasts. Dr. Irvin Wolkoff, a Toronto psychiatrist, confirms that women who go under the knife so that they can look different are almost certain to have problems with self-esteem. Brit Lisa Connell was diagnosed with an inoperable brain tumour in 2006, and as a lifelong fan of the *Ghost* beauty Demi Moore, wants to splash $60,000 on surgery to transform herself into a Moore look-a-like. On her Twitter page, the star Demi Moore writes, "Wish I could contact this woman Lisa Connell who wants to have surgery to look like me and encourage her to not to! She is a beautiful girl!" Moore is reported to have undergone a body overhaul in 2004 – allegedly spending $308,000 on a head-to-toe surgical makeover.

We are not here to put the blame on women. We have no control over what women will wear in public and how they present their bodies. We are not here to start a movement to eradicate pornography. Pornography is a sign and symptom of a unhealthy world. The only control we have here is to recognize our own responsibility to pursue purity—inwardly and outwardly, at home and in the marketplace—in the midst of a hyper-sexualized culture.

The following is a true or false self-assessment to see how well you behave in terms of sexual purity in our hyper-sexualized world. If you believe this self-assessment speaks to you and convicts your heart, please call a doctor, a counselor, or your pastor and seek professional help.

SEXUAL ADDICTION
SELF ASSESSMENT (SASA)

1. T/F When I sit or stand in front of a woman, I frequently find it difficult to keep my eyes above her neckline.

2. T/F When I look at a woman who is wearing a blouse, I want to look sideways into the gap between her buttons to see part of her bra or to see whether she is wearing a bra.

3. T/F When I look at a woman, I want to focus on her breasts first.

4. T/F When I walk by a woman who is wearing a pair of summer shorts and is sitting down with her legs spread out, I want to look or focus between her thighs.

5. T/F When a woman who is wearing clothing with low neckline bends down, I automatically want to look down to see her bra and/or her cleavage.

6. T/F When a woman wears clothing with a low neckline, my eyes want to focus on her cleavage.

7. T/F In public places, such as a mall, I have deliberately followed women who physically attract my attention.

8. T/F On public beaches, my eyes are very busy watching women who wear revealing swimwear.

9. T/F When comes to watching women in a sexual way,

church is no longer a safe place for me, i.e., I have looked at women sexually in the church.

10. T/F   Privately, I watch Sex TV or Sex File on TV at night when my family is asleep.

11. T/F   Privately, I scan the CBC French channel and cable movies on Showcase with the hope of catching something sexually exciting or distracting.

12. T/F   I have looked at soft porn men's magazines in drugstores and gas stations.

13. T/F   I have started looking at porn magazines and websites in my early teen years.

14. T/F   Pornographic materials were available in my childhood home.

15. T/F   Privately (at home or work), I have looked at, cruised on, and/or downloaded pornographic material (soft or hard) on the Internet.

16. T/F   Privately, I have a pattern of viewing Internet pornography (soft or hard) and then masturbating to the computer screen, after which the pornographic images become gross and dirty, and I turn off the Internet

17. T/F   Privately, I have a pattern of watching soft or hard core porn DVDs and masturbating to the TV screen, after which the pornographic images become gross and dirty and I return the DVDs.

18. T/F   Images in lingerie catalogues (e.g., Victoria Secret) arouse me, and I take the catalogue to the bathroom and masturbate while looking at the pictures of the lingerie models.

19. T/F   I frequently want to have sex with my wife and/or make sexual advances toward her.

20. T/F   I frequently have sexual advances toward my girlfriend/fiancé.

21. T/F   In lovemaking with my wife, I have wanted her to pose, act, or wear something in a way similar to the images I've seen on the Internet or the DVD/movie/magazine.

22. T/F   In lovemaking with my wife, I have a strong interest or fixation on her breasts and very often sucks her breasts and nipples like an infant seeking mother's milk for soothing comfort, bonding, and security.

23. T/F   In lovemaking with my wife, I have a strong interest or fixation on her buttock and very often prefer the come from behind, doggie style position on the marriage bed.

24. T/F   Privately, I have watched hard-core, adult pornographic DVDs and movies on the Internet.

25. T/F   Privately, I have watched pornography that depicts violence on women.

26. T/F   Privately, I have watched gay pornography.

27. T/F   I have or used to have subscriptions to adult pornographic materials (books, magazines, DVD, Internet porn sites).

28. T/F   I have watched and collected child pornography and/or participated in sexual relationships on the Internet with pre-teen and teenage girls on the Internet.

29. T/F   Privately (at home or work), I masturbate quite regularly, e.g., 3-5 times a week or more.

30. T/F   When I masturbate, the visual images I use to assist my masturbation belong to women other than my wife.

31. T/F   I have secretly picked up underwear of female friends/relatives and have masturbated with the underwear.

32. T/F   Privately (at home or work), I have participated in

sexual chat rooms on the Internet, e-mail/instant message communications, Facebook, or text messages with someone who interests me sexually or romantically.

33. T/F   When I drive by someone's town house or condo at night, I want to look in the bedroom and/or bathroom windows.

34. T/F   I had pre-marital sex or heavy petting before marriage.

35. T/F   I had committed extra-marital affairs in the past or virtual/e-affairs with someone on the Internet.

36. T/F   I have paid to see a strip show, hired an escort/prostitute, or attended massage parlors.

37. T/F   I have been tempted to call escort services in the Yellow Pages.

38. T/F   I have been tempted to talk to or pick up a prostitute on the street.

39. T/F   I grew up in a home where my mom and/or dad showed very little or restricted emotional connection and physical affection.

40. T/F   I have or used to have problems controlling my anger, e.g., my anger can turn into a rage very quickly.

41. T/F   For many years, I have battled with low self-esteem, insecurity, fear, and a sense of failure.

42. T/F   I have an inner sense of being inadequate, not good enough, not measured up, and unworthy as a human being.

43. T/F   I have been told that I am a controlling, intense person who tends to be a perfectionist and takes things seriously and personally.

44. T/F   I don't have a male friend to privately talk about things that bother me.

45. T/F   I don't know how to relax and have fun, or I have a

hard time coping with stress.

46. **T/F** For many years I have been serving God in the church but privately no one know about my double life, my struggles with pornography, and viewing women in sexualized ways.

47. **T/F** I have been lying to myself and others, keeping secret my involvement with pornography or sexual chat rooms, and viewing women as sexual objects.

48. **T/F** I have experienced many broken promises to myself and to my spouse/fiancé/girlfriend when comes to wanting to stop my struggles and addiction to pornography.

49. **T/F** I love my wife and children very much but I don't think they understand me.

50. **T/F** Frequently, I avoid resolving or don't know how to resolve fights and conflicts with my wife/girlfriend.

51. **T/F** I have a strong tendency to internalize my thoughts and feelings.

52. **T/F** I have a very hard time handling rejection, criticism, mistakes, and failures.

53. **T/F** I have a strong yearning for approval, acceptance, and affirmation from people.

DISSECTING THE MIND OF A MAN WHO VIEWS WOMEN AS SEXUAL OBJECTS

The mind of a man who frequently objectifies women sexually is like a computer hard drive full of files and folders of sexual nature. Here is how his mind works:

- Each sexual/visual image of a woman and her body becomes a file in his mind.

- The files together form a folder in the mind.
- The folder represents the package of women attractive to the man. The package is soothing, comforting, pleasant, attractive, and sexually arousing to the man.
- When the man looks at women in public, he searches for the same package stored in his mind folder.
- He doesn't look at any or every woman; instead he looks for a particular woman who matches the package of images in his mind.
- When the man finds a woman who fits the package, his eyes fall on her, follow her, and look at her, usually as a sexual object.

THE FUNCTIONS AND IMPACTS OF PORNOGRAPHY ON A MAN'S LIFE

It is a myth that pornography is about sex. It is another myth that pornography is useful to resurrect deteriorating sex life within a marriage. Like crack cocaine, pornography is a highly addictive drug that men use to run away from all kinds of pain and problems.

1. PORNOGRAPHY IS NOT ABOUT SEX. IT IS ABOUT THE EXPERIENCE OF:

- Restoring control
- Restoring power
- Seeking purpose, acceptance, and approval
- Soothing and comforting the mind and body
- Relieving stress and tension
- Running away from pain, problems, and reality
- Emotional and chemical satisfaction

2. Pornography is a drug/psychological medication to seek relief from:

- The pain of rejection
- The pain of insecurity
- The pain of shame
- The pain of not receiving respect
- The pain of failures
- The pain of abandonment
- The pain of boredom and loneliness
- The pain of being misunderstood
- The pain of not feeling accepted
- The pain of not receiving approval

3. Pornography is addictive and abusive to our body

- When a man is sexually aroused by watching pornographic materials and subsequent masturbation, the man's pain-killing centre in his mid-brain is activated during peak arousal. Signals from this part of his brain instruct his body to release endorphins and corticosteroids, which can temporarily numb physical and emotional pain, as well as reduce anxiety, ease fear, and have a calming effect. A man has to hold onto his genital when he masturbates, and he has every control and power with his hand to orchestrate the masturbation experience. Just like putting himself back in the driver's seat, the man regains a sense of control and power, and physiologically experiences a calming effect.

- God created sex for husband and wife to enjoy its pleasure, arousal, and intimacy. Sex is a great and healthy gift from God to be enjoyed within His will, i.e., within the boundary of marriage. Contemporary studies show that sexual arousal and an active sex life may lead to a longer life, better heart health, an improved ability to ward off pain, a more robust immune system, lower rates of depression, and even protection against certain cancers. These are heavenly blessings of God-created sex for married couples, which leave its mark not just on the mind, but on the body as well. The release of endorphins and corticosteroids during sexual arousal and intimacy between husband and wife on the marriage bed is a blessing from God and within His will. Sex within God's intelligent design is good for our physical, emotional, and spiritual health.

- Sexual arousal and releasing of pain-killing agents endorphin and corticosteroids by means of pornography and masturbation are not within the will of God. It is a form of abusing the biochemical resources of the physical body and medicating oneself outside God's will and His intelligent design.

The Bible is very clear on how sexual sins affect our body. All sin is equal in the sense of eternal ramifications, but not all sin is equal in its earthly ramifications.

The apostle Paul writes, "Shun immorality and all sexual looseness (flee from impurity in thought, word, or deed). Any other sin, which a man commits, is one outside the body, but he who commits sexual immorality sins against his own body. Do you not know that your body is the temple (the very sanctuary) of the Holy Spirit who lives within you, whom you have received (as a gift) from God? You are not your own. You were bought with a price (purchased with preciousness and paid for, made His own). So then, honor God and bring glory to Him in your body." (1Corinthians 6:18-20, the Amplified Bible)

King Solomon writes, "Be not wise in your own eyes;

reverently fear and worship the Lord and turn (entirely) away from evil. It shall be health to your nerves and sinews, and marrow and moistening to your bones." (Proverbs 3: 7-8, the Amplified Bible)

4. FREQUENT OR RECREATIONAL USE OF PORNOGRAPHY IS NOT VICTIMLESS

- It induces feelings and actions of uncleanness
- It carries long-term effects: Experts say men who frequently view porn may develop unrealistic expectations of women's appearance and behaviors, have difficulty in forming and sustaining relationships, and difficulty in feeling sexually satisfied.
- It is highly addictive and breeds shame. The more pornography is consumed, the more the addiction grows.
- It gives rise to the belief that "pornography is common, hurts no one, and is socially acceptable, and the female body is for male entertainment."
- It does not teach communication, emotional connection, healthy body beliefs, and expected time on foreplay, arousal, orgasm, and intimacy.
- According to Dr. Mary Anne Layden, a University of Pennsylvania psychotherapist who testified before the US Senate on the dangers of online pornography, there has not been one case of sexual violence she worked on that did not involve pornography. Robert Burgoyne, a Toronto-based sex therapist, said in the June 2008 edition of *Maclean's* magazine that the danger with pornography in general is that it encourages users to isolate sexuality from emotional intimacy. It becomes problematic if it interferes with other aspects of life such as school, work, and relationships or if the users are getting harmful information or locked into objectifying women sexually.

- According to Jennifer Schneider, co-author of *Cybersex Exposed: Simple Fantasy or Obsession*, the Internet is the crack cocaine of sexual addiction.

5. PORNOGRAPHY AND DIVORCE

- At the 2003 meeting of the American Academy of Matrimonial Lawyers, a majority of the 350 lawyers who attended said the Internet played a significant role in divorces in the past year, with excessive interest in online pornography contributing to more than half of the cases (*Time Magazine*, Canadian Edition, February 9, 2004).

6. PORNOGRAPHY AND SEX ON THE MARRIAGE BED

- If real-world healthy sex on the marriage bed were a meal, the chicken would be at times not hot enough and there would not be quite enough dessert to go around. If real-world sex on the marriage bed were a house, the plumbing would be at times not working well, especially when the house is getting older or facing a storm. Pornography, on the other hand, is all about the fantasy of abundance. It is like a fairy-tale feast where the chicken is always hot, the food is perfectly prepared, there are plenty of desserts to go around, and there is more than enough for everyone. Even better, the diners did not have to work or cook it – it was no work or trouble at all. For the house, the plumbing always works. The tap does not drip, the pipe does not freeze, and the water supply does not stop. If pornography were a feast to consume, it is a myth that it is an adult entertainment for the grown-ups. The idea that sex and sexuality can be reduced to fixed components as it is in pornography – oral sex, anal sex, doggie style, fake breasts, money shot, girl-on-girl – is adolescent: 1st base, 2nd base, immature all the way. Pornography is designed for someone to run away to the fantasy world like a kid.

7. Pornography Hurts Women

- When spouses are addicted to pornography, the emotional tolls it takes on loved ones is like having a severe, sometimes fatal, relationship injury. The injury destroys the vital attachment bond between a man and a woman. The attachment injury comes with emotional pain, distrust, and a sense of abandonment. In many cases, the loved ones no longer believe they can count on their spouses to be there for them.

- For many women who discover their husbands, fiancés, or boyfriends involved in pornography, the discovery of the pornography is often seen as a betrayal and even as adultery, and they feel like they are not good enough. A wife wrote, "My husband has rejected me, been deceptive, abandoned me and the kids, lied to me. He has never apologized for the destruction and devastation the pornography has brought into the marriage. He has not been truthful about who he is, and he has broken our marriage vows that he would be faithful to me alone. I look at pornography as being unfaithful because he will hide himself from me and run to the pornography."

A WOMAN FINDING OUT

In the fall of 2003, I was 20 years old and I had been dating a guy named Matt for two years. Matt and I were in love and happy, yet we had some issues. Matt had some bad habits that I did not like and it caused us to have some serious fights. Matt was a guy who often watched pornography and masturbated to it. This habit of his made me very jealous, and I lost a lot of my confidence. Finally I told Matt that if he did not cut down and eventually stop, it would be over for us.

Matt decided he would cut down altogether. Instead of looking at the very bold pornography, Matt was going to try looking at soft porn and hoped this would eventually help him stop. Months and months went by, and I still had this feeling that something was not right. Whenever I questioned him, he always had the perfect answer for me.

Finally, on the night of December 7, 2003, Matt told the truth. His exact words were, "Lisa, I have been lying to you. These past months when you thought I was not looking at a lot of porn and masturbating much, it was all a lie. I have been looking at the dirty stuff and masturbating to it, more often then I should have."

I could not believe what I had just heard. This could not be true, I felt so angry but mostly betrayed. I even slapped Matt across the face. My whole life felt like it was falling apart—this guy whom I had loved and trusted had been lying to me for months. "How could he do this to me?" I thought to myself. "How can he say he loves me?" I felt so betrayed and hurt, and I hated Matt for what he had done. I started yelling at him; to me he was nothing but a shallow pervert. At the same time I felt like I was no good and that I was the reason why he turned to images of other women to satisfy himself. I kept trying to figure out what I had done wrong as a girlfriend. I kept thinking maybe if I was prettier or had a sexier body he would not have done this. I finally asked him why. He said he didn't know, that he wanted to stop but the temptation was so strong, and he did not know how to fight it. The next day Matt and I talked about it some more. We fought and talked, and Matt kept telling me how sorry he was and how he did not mean to hurt me. Even though I was mad about him lying I could not figure out why he just could not give up on porn.

Matt and I later got into another big fight, and after yelling and yelling at each other, I locked both of us in a room until we calmed down and could figure out what was really going on with him. That is when it hit Matt—he finally realized what he was doing needed to stop. I realized this habit of Matt's went a lot deeper than I thought.

7. ADDICTION TO PORNOGRAPHY AND VIEWING WOMEN AS SEXUAL OBJECTS IS ONE OF THE BIGGEST AND MOST SECRETIVE PROBLEMS OF CHRISTIAN MEN (PASTORS, LEADERS, MISSIONARIES, MARRIED AND SINGLE MEN) FACING THE CHURCH TODAY.

According to Promise Keepers, 65 percent of the men polled indicated they struggle with pornography (*Unchained*, Pure Life Ministries, winter 2002, p.4). In a 2001 survey published in *Leadership Journal*, 37 percent of pastors said pornography was a struggle for them, and 51 percent admitted it was a temptation.

> *"Dear Dr. Sheh, thank you for the participation you were involved in on television with Paul Arthur on the Miracle Channel today. I had served as a pastor for a number of years and went through a burnout in 2002 which took me out of ministry. A Christian psychologist was very helpful in assisting me through the recovery process. While I am not pastoring at this time it has been a blessing to get back on my feet again. The struggle that I had with pornography while still in the pastoral ministry was immense. No one knew what I was doing though and you are the only one that I have shared this with. The chemistry factor involved with pornography that brings a release to the stress and depression that I was dealing while going through some difficult church issues as a pastor is a very real thing. You have spelled it out so clearly to me on the program this morning. May God bless you as you continue to minister so openly regarding this growing plague in our society."*

From a Canadian pastor

"We are looking for somewhere to send a couple with acute marriage problems... Strongholds need to be broken and the marriage restored. It is a critical situation... women are so oppressed and a large percentage depressed here. Teaching our missionaries and pastors could be very freeing for these first generation Christians and on into future before the accessibility of pornography becomes rampant in rural areas.

You have heard my pleas from the field for my comrades – as you said pornography, adultery, marital discord. It is definitely a battle field and for me it seems that, with vigor, satan pulls out every stronghold he can to destroy the missionary and to send them home with their tale between their legs... Satan uses the strongholds to make the missionary ineffective. The missionary feels too vulnerable to share with trained counselors who are rare on the mission field – and may make one neither go home and face huge ramifications, nor share with fellow missionaries because it is letting the side down, being a burden, showing one is incompetent, weak. Therefore when there is a problem it goes too long without help. Then it becomes a huge drain on the resources on the field."

From a former missionary in Asia

THE ADDICTIVE CYCLE
OF PORNOGRAPHY

Like any addiction, pornography affects men in a predicative cycle:

- The man is experiencing pain (e.g., feeling rejected, insecurity, losing control, losing purpose, boredom, looking for excitement, etc.) and sowing seeds of discontent in his mind.
- The man is vulnerable, and his mind/body is looking for pain relief and comfort.
- The sexual files in his mind become active and search,

chase, and hunt for matches to his package.

- The man's eyes and mind intensify the focus on viewing women as sexual objects, both publicly and privately.
- The man's conscience sends out moral resistance.
- The man's internal agitation increases.
- The man succumbs to the strong desire for pain relief by renting a soft-porn DVD or going into a porn site on the Internet.
- The sexual files in his mind search for the right packages of women and images to facilitate the best release of tension and restoration of power, control, and soothing comfort.
- The man masturbates to the porn images and experiences the relief (short-term).
- The sexual files in the man's mind obtain the matches and de-activate.
- The man's mind/body no longer looks for pain relief and the images and activities on the DVD/Internet become gross, dirty, and immoral in his eyes.
- The man returns the DVD or turn off the Internet site.
- The above same cycle returns the next time the man feels vulnerable.

LISTEN TO AN (COCAINE) ADDICT'S CONFESSION

"I was beyond helping myself. Thank goodness some friends stepped in… I've never met a happy cocaine addict. Every addict is, by definition, running away from a thousand different kinds of pain, and using drugs or booze to make the pain disappear, which only makes it worse… There is no known cure for addiction, and what makes its hold so strong on us is that it's a physical, mental and spiritual disease rolled into one… In fact, nearly all

addicts are alone – they push everyone away to be with their drug. This is what I mean about addiction being a spiritual disease. It cuts you off from everyone and disconnects you from any sense of belonging… Addiction can only be halted by reconnecting addicts to their feelings and their community. Without that connection, the addiction will continue unabated."

Similarly, in sexual addiction, pornography and images of women as sexual objects are used as a high-powered drug for pain relief. Therefore, sexual addiction is not just a moral and spiritual issue; it is a health matter that affects many people's lives.

"I went to Bible school and felt a call to the ministry. All the while, I struggled periodically with looking at porn. It gave me a sense of acceptance. In the fantasy world I escaped to, I was in control. I would never be rejected. I was thoroughly accepted, significant, and important. This is what I didn't feel in the 'real' world…I took my first ministry assignment. Disappointment crept in; there were many demands from competing interest groups. I had little support from my senior pastor. I began to feel defeated, rejected, alone, misunderstood, vulnerable. I found myself unable to connect authentically with anyone – my wife, my family, the leadership at church, not even God. I again turned to comforting myself in the fantasy world, craving the sense of freedom from shame…Except that the shame always returned and intensified. I'd give in to temptation and then realize I was lying, covering up, afraid of being discovered. It became a swirling vortex of one lie, one sin after another. The cycle of rationalizing, promising myself I'd stop, confessing to God, repenting, cleaning up my act and then getting sucked right back under was becoming a bizarre, twisted kind of psychological medication to me."

From *It's All About Grace*
Good Hope, Vol. 3, Issue 1, Spring 2006
Clergy Care Network, Focus on the Family (Canada)

"After having been "found out" about my porn use, almost 3 years ago, I went though a spiritual healing with a Christian counselor, who helped me to discover a life long fear about maternal abandonment, which probably even extended to a fear about abandonment by any females dear to me, especially my wife... wrongly, of course, even though I was a believing Christian, I turned to porn... the lifelong fear, I learned, was borne out of vision I was helped to recall, of my mother, very angrily, throwing me into my crib as an infant and screaming very loudly and angrily... not understanding the words, may have been a blessing, but the sentiment, nonetheless, stayed with me... and I obviously made a very bad decision to "self-medicate" the way I did... I think, the fact that I used porn as a "pain killer," not as a "high," that I am less likely to go back to it... it was never about sex for me, it was about acceptance (I know it was false, but...). Jesus healed the hurt in my heart over my mother and I no longer feel the simmering fear/pain in the background... i.e., the pain is gone... I am not so foolish to not think that Satan will continue to try to attack and I do want to stay pure in thought and deed, but I believe, that, greater is He!"

From a Canadian professional

CHAPTER THREE

KNOWING
YOUR ENEMY

A slick campaign of propaganda is spreading an insane apologia of evil, a senseless cult of Satan. Bodies are constantly bought and sold on the streets of our cities, on our television channels, in homes that have become like streets.

Pope Benedict XVI

Satan has no weapon of mass destruction. Satan's grand scheme is to strike down God's children *one man at a time.*

SATAN ADVANCES HIS
BATTLE PLAN BY:

1. LIES AND DECEPTION: SATAN IS THE GREATEST "CON MAN" AND MASTER OF DECEPTION

Where did the term "con man" come from? It's more than

160 years old. On July 8, 1849, the *New York Herald* reported the arrest of a swindler named William Thompson. Mr. Thompson would approach his mark by saying, "Sir, do I have your confidence?" and then penetrate his scam. The newspaper headlined the story "The Arrest of the Confidence Man."

SATAN'S DECEPTION #1:

Gain your confidence, even if it's just for a moment.

- "Just one look for a moment" (Underrating the power of our flesh – another sexual file created in the mind).
- "Just one glance for a moment" (Underrating the power of our flesh – another sexual file created in the mind).
- "Just follow the woman for a moment" (Underrating the power of vulnerability).
- "Just for a moment. It does no harm" (Satan's deception).
- "Just for a moment. It's victimless" (Satan's deception).
- "Just for a moment. You can handle it" (Overrating our own strength).
- "It's okay for just a moment. God would forgive you" (Check out Romans 6:1-14).
- "Just for a moment. This is the only way to relieve your tension and regain control" (it is Satan's lies to put all your eggs in one basket).

SATAN'S DECEPTION #2:

You can always ask God for forgiveness and God will always love you.

Satan would only label a pornography problem as a moral and spiritual issue. Addiction to pornography is more than a

moral and spiritual issue, it is a health problem. Our God is
Jehovah Rophe, the Lord who heals our diseases. God is more
than our saviour, He is our physician and counselor.

> *"It was a major revelation that Porn is a health issue!"*
>
> Former Pure at Heart seminar attendee

> *"Thank you so much for your obedience in coming to Calgary
> this weekend! The seminar was exactly what I needed today. I
> have struggled off and on with pornography and unhealthy views
> of women as sex objects for years, but have never gotten a hold
> of the concept of how I could gain the Victory until today. Not
> only did you provide the information about the destruction that
> pornography can do to us as men, but you provided the tools for us
> to gain the Victory as well! My eyes were really opened when you
> talked about Satan saying that we can always go for forgiveness,*
> *but that is not going to break the cycle if we are going to do it over
> and over again."*
>
> Former Pure at Heart seminar attendee

2. SELLING PORNOGRAPHY AS A POWERFUL ADDICTIVE DRUG TO:

- Medicate our fears
- Medicate our insecurity
- Medicate our inadequacy
- Medicate our feeling of rejection and lack of respect
- Medicate our disappointments
- Medicate our desire for control
- Medicate our desire for approval and affirmation
- Medicate our loneliness, boredom, and stress

> *Satan is the master salesman and drug pusher.*

3. Abusing our God-given natural pain killers (endorphins and corticosteroids) outside of God's will and plan

- Satan knows how our mind and body works.
- Satan knows how the neurochemistry of endorphins and corticosteroids work in our brain to numb pain and calm fear.
- Satan knows that we want a quick fix, a magic pill to ease our pain.
- Satan knows that when people are in pain, they want to escape reality. Looking at manufactured cleavages, breasts, and bodies on the Internet triggers the release of endorphins and corticosteroids and is a way to escape reality and run away from pain.
- Satan knows North America is big business for the drug industry because many of us want some sort of medication to quickly ease our pain (In Canada, more than 361 million drug prescriptions was recorded in 2003).

Satan is the master abuser.

4. Saturating our world with easily accessible hyper-sexualized images in popular culture and in the privacy of a home, office, or hotel room

- As of July 2003, there were 260 million pages of pornography online - an increase of 1800 percent since 1998. Porn amounts to about 7 percent of the 3.3 billion web pages indexed by *Google*.
- Internet users who access adult websites spend an average of 73 minutes per month there, but that doesn't include time spent on amateur porn sites.
- Americans rent upwards of 800 million pornography

videos and DVDs a year, compared with 3.6 billion non-pornographic videos. Nearly one in five rentals is a porn flick.

- Hollywood produces 400 feature films a year. The porn industry churns out 11,000.

- In Japan, the June 2008 edition of the *Time* Magazine reported that the country has seen a surging demand for pornography that has turned adult videos into a billion-dollar industry, with "elder porn" one of its fastest growing genres. Shigeo Tokuda (his stage name), 73, has appeared in some 350 adult films over the past 14 years.

- One in four American adults surveyed in 2002 admitted to seeing an X-rated movie in the past year.

- 34 percent of Internet users visited adult websites in 2005.

- In early 2007, 48 percent of US visitors to adult websites were women.

- 35 percent of 8th grade boys in Alberta, Canada, say they have viewed Internet porn "too many times to count." 8 percent of 8th grade girls say the same. Most of the boys and almost half of the girls who have seen porn say they logged on deliberately.

- Average age when California high school boys first see porn: eleven. Average age when California high school girls first see porn: twelve. 41 percent of California high school boys and girls thought their run-ins with online porn were "no big deal."

- According to a survey by a U.S. family-planning organization, published in December 2009, 20 percent of American teenagers said they had participated in sexting, a combination of the words "sex" and "texting," a way of youths exchanging nude photos of themselves over cell phones.

- Sex sells in sports. Shaune Bagwell, ex-wife of Houston Astro star Jeff Bagwell, sold her cleavage for $15,000 US on eBay. Concerned parents in the United States are livid because the *Sports Illustrated* swimsuit issue is corrupting America's youth, reported Mike Bianchi of the *Orlando Sentinel*. In sports, the female body is a valuable commodity, a product to be sold like any other. In London, England the tabloid press during Wimbledon seems to prefer skin over athleticism.

- Sex is sold to kids. According to Cathy Wing of Media-Awareness, a non-profit educational organization for media literacy, the fashion industry has been using increasingly younger models and now commonly portrays 13- and 14-year olds as "men" and "women" who sell adult sexuality in fashion ads. The increased sexualization of pre-teens in fashion advertising and popular culture reinforces the belief that it is acceptable to treat children as sexual commodities.

- Sex sells in Canada. *The National Post* reported on February 12, 2005 that distributors of adult cable and satellite programming are responding to consumer demand in a culture where hard-core porn is increasingly mainstream and such adult stars as Jenna Jameson publish memoirs and enter into contracts to produce "moan tones" for wireless phones. The adult sector is profitable for the cable and satellite distributors because their share is as much as 70 percent of every subscriber dollar, according to an industry insider. Sun Media reported in January 2009 that hundreds, if not thousands, of porn videos are produced in Toronto every year, feeding a growing appetite in Canada of homegrown adult entertainment. Local porn producers rank Toronto as the second or third largest Canadian hub in the country after Montreal and Vancouver. While not yet on par with either of those cities, or the continent's porn capital in Los Angeles, Toronto has a large and growing porn industry, one that is largely invisible and self-regulated.

- In Canada, *The National Post* reported that Rogers is the most aggressive distributor in offering "consumer choice" in the adult field. In addition to the five adult subscription channels currently available, Rogers offers video-on-demand programming and as many as eight pay-per-view adult channels. Bell ExpressVu offers 11 pay-per-view adult channels, marketed under its own "Venus" brand. The Movie Network, owned by Astral Media Inc. in Montreal has become the only mainstream English-language movie channel to offer explicit XXX-rated films to cable and satellite subscribers in Eastern Canada. According to senior management at Astral Television Networks, this is a natural progression in the changing standards of Canadian television viewers. Ashley Corsiatto, vice-president for marketing of Real Productions, the Alberta, Sherwood Park-based adult video company, said in an August 2008 *Sun Media* entertainment interview that porn does not have the same stigma it did years ago… It is a legitimate business with legitimate business opportunities.

- At the four-star Grand Hotel and Suites in Toronto, freedom of expression is found in a TV set, with guests enjoying "free" access to two 24-hour adult entertainment channels. The cost is built into the room rates.

- Sex and nudity has been unnoticeably creeping into the video games industry. Blood Rayne originally a video game with explicit nudity that features a character of the same name now appears in Playboy as a sexualized illustration. The game BMX: XXX shows explicit nudity. Grand Theft Auto: San Andreas and The Sims 2, two popular video games, can both be "molded" to show naked characters. Brad Adam, a Vancouver entrepreneur, is marketing Virtually Jenna, a photo-realistic and explicit video game featuring adult star Jenna Jameson.

Satan is the master marketer.

As a master con man, a drug pusher, an abuser, and a deceptive marketer, Satan is cashing in on his business. His battle plan is working.

Do you want to pursue purity, gain victory over pornography, and stop viewing women as sexual objects? If yes, you need to know the way your mind and body work, and the deceptions that Satan uses to advance his battle plan.

CHAPTER FOUR

LIFE TIME PURE AT HEART TOOLS FOR HEALTHY AND GODLY LIVING

A 3-STEP APPROACH TO GAIN VICTORY OVER SEXUAL STRONGHOLDS WITH PORNOGRAPHY AND VIEWING WOMEN AS SEXUAL OBJECTS:

1. DE-FILE
2. DE-CYCLE
3. RE-WIRE

DE-FILE

STRATEGY #1

DE-FILE BY DE-ACTIVATING THE SEXUAL FILES IN THE MIND.

DE-ACTIVATE THE SEXUAL FILES BY PUTTING ALL IMAGES ASSOCIATED WITH WOMEN AS SEXUAL OBJECTS "UNDER THE BAN."

BIBLICAL STORY & STRATEGY: THE JOSHUA PRINCIPLE

So Joshua smote all the land, the hill country, the South, the lowland, and the slopes, and all their kings. He left none remaining, but utterly destroyed all that breathed, as the Lord, the God of Israel, commanded. (Joshua 10:40, the Amplified Bible).

ACHAN: THE SIN OF VULNERABILITY (JOSHUA 6-8)

JOSHUA 6: THE VICTORY AT JERICHO AND GOD'S INSTRUCTION

- V.17, except for Rahab the harlot and her household, and the silver, gold, bronze and iron that went into the treasury of the Lord, the city should be "under God's herem, or under the ban." That is, Jericho was devoted to God for total destruction. It was impossible for pure faith and worship to be maintained in Israel except by the complete elimination of the Canaanites themselves who practiced religious prostitution and infant sacrifice.

JOSHUA 7: THE SIN OF ACHAN AND THE DEFEAT AT AI

- V.1, Achan: he *saw*, he *coveted*, and he *took*. (Eve took the same steps in the Garden of Eden; David took the same steps with Bathsheba; you and I take the same steps in our sexual temptations).
- V.21, Achan took a beautiful robe from Babylonia, 200 shekels of silver, and a 50-shekel wedge of gold.
- God's anger burned against the sons of Israel. With Israel underestimating the power of their enemy at Ai, and over-estimating their own strength, they were defeated at Ai.

- Achan and his family were stoned to death. God then turned from the fierceness of His anger.

JOSHUA 8: VICTORY AT AI

The spoil of Ai and also its livestock could be taken by Israel. Note: Jericho had been "under the ban" but Ai was not.

LESSONS TO BE LEARNED FROM THE SINS OF ACHAN AND THE BATTLES AT JERICHO AND AI:

- The Joshua principle: all things associated with sexual immorality and sexual looseness is "under the ban" – under God's herem, devoted to God for complete destruction.
- Safeguard against Satan's lies, lest we underestimate the power of our flesh, or overestimate our strength, or assume that one victory guarantees another. Yesterday's victory does not make a believer immune from defeat today. Ai was not "under the ban." If only Achan had suppressed his greedy and selfish desires and obeyed God's word at Jericho, he would later have had all his heart desired and God's blessing too. Similarly, if we discipline ourselves and shun immorality and all sexual looseness (flee from impurity in thought, word, or deed), God will bless our sexual desire within marriage or with our future mate.
- After failure comes a second chance. One defeat or failure does not signal the end of a believer's usefulness for God.
- The path of obedience and faith is always best. This path also contains God's ways to gain peace and restore control in our lives. When there is no peace in our heart, there are battles in our mind. Our mind's battles give us wear and tear and make us vulnerable to Satan's lies. We subsequently succumb to sexual sins in a cycle of short-lived control.

DE-FILE HOMEWORK #1

PUT ALL IMAGES ASSOCIATED WITH WOMEN AS SEXUAL OBJECTS "UNDER THE BAN" OR DEVOTE THEM TO GOD FOR TOTAL DESTRUCTION.

Total destruction of images of sexual objects in your home and office (images contained in magazines, newspapers, CD covers, DVDs, movies, satellite), leaving none remaining.

- Cut them up.
- Shred them.
- Tear them up.
- Throw them away outside of your home.
- Stop the subscription.
- Read the DVD rating labels and content. Do not rent DVD with ratings that contain sexual contents, nudity, and explicit sexual scenes. Leaving a video store empty handed is not a disappointment—it is a celebration because none of the DVDs you want fit your standard. Remember, God wants you to be a godly man, not just a Christian man.
- Treat yourself like an alcoholic who cannot even have a drop of alcohol. You cannot allow yourself to view just for a moment any images and body cues in your environment that are associated with women as sexual objects and soothing comfort; otherwise you are trapped again in Satan's deception.

DE-FILE HOMEWORK #2

DO NOT UNDERESTIMATE THE POWER OF SATAN'S LIES AND DECEPTION

- Do not underrate the power of your flesh (the sexual files in your mind always want to activate and look for the package matches).
- Do not underrate the power of your vulnerability to seek pain relief.

- Do not overestimate your strengths to resist Satan, the master con man.
- Persistently and consistently devote all images of sexual objects to total destruction. Do not add new files to your folder. Put them "under the ban." Make it a strong and life long habit.

STRATEGY #2

DE-ACTIVATE THE SEXUAL FILES BY NEUTRALIZING THE POWER OF VIEWING WOMEN AS SEXUAL OBJECTS

"For this is the will of God, that you should be consecrated (separated and set apart for pure and holy living): that you should abstain and shrink from all sexual vice (porneia, translated "sexual immorality," namely adultery, premarital and extramarital intercourse, homosexuality, and other sexual looseness)"

(1Thessalonians 4:3, the Amplified Bible)

"Shun immorality and all sexual looseness (flee from impurity in thought, word, or deed)."

(1 Corinthians 6:18a, the Amplified Bible)

"I dictated a covenant (an agreement) to my eyes; how then could I look (lustfully) upon a girl?"

(Job 31:1, the Amplified Bible)

HOW TO NEUTRALIZE THE POWER OF VIEWING WOMEN AS SEXUAL OBJECTS:

- Rehearse to yourself the word "neutralize."
- Whenever you want to look at a woman as a sexual object (refer to examples on your self-assessment), say to yourself the word "neutralize" and turn your eyes away. Look at objects neutral to sexual seduction – a piece of furniture, an office sign, the window, a decoration, etc.

- Rehearse to yourself "this woman is God's creation, not a sexual object" and continue the neutralizing process.
- When you spot a woman "miles ahead" that fits the package in your mind, bring up the word "neutralize," start looking at neutralized objects, and let the woman be gone from your sight.
- Prepare yourself to neutralize in "sexual objects hot spots," such as the beach, the park in summer time, and the summer season when you see more women with tank tops, bikini, shorts, sundresses, and flip-flops.
- Stay away from and keep your eyes away from newsstands that sell soft porn men's magazines. If you want to read other magazines, take the magazines and read them somewhere away from the newsstands that have soft porn men's magazines in their display.
- The strategy of neutralization requires discipline and persistency. Practice neutralization often so that it becomes a strong and life long habit.
- The more you practice the method of neutralization, the more you find that sexual objects and packages lose their power.

DE-FILE HOMEWORK #3

BEGIN THE HABIT OF NEUTRALIZATION AND MASTER THIS TECHNIQUE IN PUBLIC PLACES

- In the bank in front of the female teller.
- In a store in front of the female sale representative.
- In the shoe store when the female clerk knee down to fit your new shoes.
- In the gym full of women doing exercises.
- Before the red traffic light when a woman walks by.
- In the church when you see a woman who fits your package walk by or sing with the worship team or choir.

- In the office when you mingle with female co-workers who fit your package.
- In the small group when there are women present who fit your package.
- Identify other places such as _____

DE-CYCLE

STRATEGY

DE-CYCLE THE ADDICTIVE PATTERNS TO RELIEVE YOUR PAIN

So whoever cleanses himself (from what is ignoble and unclean, who separates himself from contact with contaminating and corrupting influences) will (then himself) be a vessel set apart and useful for honorable and noble purposes, consecrated and profitable to the Master, fit and ready for any good work.

(2 Timothy 2:21, the Amplified Bible)

HOW TO DE-CYCLE

- Become aware of the addictive cycle.
- Identify your addictive cycle.
- Confirm you are living with the addictive cycle.
- Ask God to remove this addictive cycle from you.
- Tell yourself not to put any eggs in this basket of cycle.
- Create other baskets to put your eggs in for the function of pain relief (the re-wiring process).
- Pray for healthy ways to relieve your pain and short circuit the addictive cycle.
- Be on the offensive. Put a major road block to short circuit or block accessibility to the addictive cycle.

HOMEWORK

- Pray to God to destroy this cycle of addictive stronghold in you.
- Pray for sharp awareness of the addictive cycle before it is too late to intervene.
- Pray that God will create circumstances to distract you from completing the addictive cycle.
- For Internet users, install a program, e.g., Safe Eyes and Covenant Eyes, to increase accountability and to block (even not 100 percent) accessibility to porn sites. For drastic measures, disconnect the Internet.
- For hard-core DVD viewers, block accessibility to the cycle by asking the video store to delete your name from the membership.
- For business travelers, before you go to your hotel room, ask the front desk to delete pay TV in your room.
- For cable and satellite dish viewers, stop subscribing to programs that contain channels that show porn materials.
- In your downtime, keep yourself busy and occupied away from area where you can easily access your computer, TV, and DVD player.
- Examine your environment. At your home, keep your desktop and laptop in an open area so that your computer work is transparent to family members.
- At your workplace, keep your office door opened. If possible, re-arrange your office furniture so that co-workers who walk by can see your computer screen.
- Display inspirational photos around the office computer screen. Family photos can serve as good reminders of the reasons to avoid sexual content at work.
- Develop healthy ways to relieve pain (begin the re-wiring process).

RE-WIRE

STRATEGY #1

LEAVE THE PORNOGRAPHY BASKET EMPTY AND CREATE OTHER HEALTHY BASKETS TO PUT YOUR EGGS IN.

Blessed be the God and Father of our Lord Jesus Christ, the father of sympathy (pity and mercy) and the God (Who is the Source) of every comfort (consolation and encouragement).

(2 Corinthians 1:3, the Amplified Bible)

The God of this people Israel selected our forefathers and made this people great and important during their stay in the land of Egypt, and then with an uplifted arm He led them out from there. And for about forty years like a fatherly nurse He cared for them in the wilderness and endured their behavior.

(Acts 13:17-18, the Amplified Bible)

"And the Lord said to Cain, Why are you angry? And why do you look sad and depressed and dejected? If you do well, will you not be accepted? And if you do not do well, sin crouches at your door; its desire is for you, but you must master it."

(Genesis 4: 6-7, the Amplified Bible)

- Detect your own mental and behavioral signs of vulnerability (e.g., cannot sleep; want to control more; want more sex from your wife; masturbate more; feeling tense; increased frequency viewing women as sexual objects; increased anger outbursts, etc.)
- Label your vulnerability. Is it about fear? Is it about insecurity? Is it about shame?
- Identify the source of your fear, anxiety, insecurity, and worries. What does your heart long for? Name and label your emotional needs. Is it about affirmation? Is it about respect? Is it about acceptance? Is it about power? What is

your pain? What are you afraid of?

- Stop being a 50-year-old man who is a boy in his emotional health. Everyone man has feelings. A man must see and believe that emotions belong in the life of a man. Seek to meet your needs and emotional self-sufficiency as an adult, not as a child. Otherwise you will forever depend on others and pornography to protect your emotional health and medicate your vulnerability. The apostle Paul said, "When I was a child, I talked like a child, I reasoned like a child; now I have become a man, I am done with childish ways and have put them aside." (I Corinthians 13:11). Consult a professional counselor or pastor on how to develop emotionally self-sufficiency as an adult.

- Practice God's presence by praying without ceasing (1Thessalonians 5:17). Praying without ceasing means you can talk to God about your stuff any time, any place, and anywhere—sometimes saying a lot, sometimes saying a little, but living every moment of life as if God is right there. After all, isn't He?

- Talk to God about your fear, anxiety, insecurity, and worries. "Externalize" them to God and see what He will say to you. Internalizing your fear, anxiety, insecurity, and worries will increase your vulnerability to fall back on the addictive cycle.

- Talk to someone you trust about your struggle with pornography. Do not keep your problem a secret. Externalizing your struggle is the first step toward healing and recovery.

- Talk to your spouse about your fear, anxiety, insecurity, and worries.

- Talk to your girlfriend/fiancé about your fear, anxiety, insecurity, and worries, but both of you have to honor and adhere to strict boundaries before marriage.

- Talk to a man whom you trust and respect about your fear, anxiety, insecurity, and worries (e.g., a pastor, a trusted friend, a colleague).

- Do not share your vulnerability, personal, and marital problems with a woman who is not your spouse or immediate family member (e.g., parent, sister).

- Persistently and consistently practice the De-File and De-Cycle Pure at Heart strategies: put sexual objects "under the ban," neutralize the power of the sexual objects, and create major road blocks to short circuit accessibility to the cycle of using sexual objects as pain relief.

- Use exercises and sports (running, walking, swimming, squash, and hockey) to clear your mind and release your endorphins.

- Be part of a small Biblical Community, such as a small group, care group, life group, or men's group in your church. Scientific research has repeatedly shown that people who have a strong tie to their faith and spiritual community are happier and healthier. Religion, after all, is not a bad word because it derives from the Latin *religio*, meaning "to bind together" – linking individuals to families, friends, and community. If you value your independence and the group experience does not jibe with you, connect yourself with an emotional mentor (e.g., a pastor, a male co-worker) you trust in a one-on-one relationship.

- Improve your self-esteem to better manage disappointments, rejection, and insecurity. Discover who you are, your strengths, your gifts, your talents, your passion, and your limitations. Express your own God-worth by using, polishing, and refining your gifts and talents, and learning to appreciate voices of blessing from God and His community, i.e., His unconditional acceptance of who you are and who you are not. If necessary, seek professional counseling to deal with personal/marital issues and/or unfinished business in your life.

RE-WIRE HOMEWORK

- Identify your mental and behavioral signs when you are vulnerable.

  _____

  _____

- The elevator tool. Take an elevator on the ground floor and go down to your basement of emotions. Open the elevator door and look around. Search, identify, and name your fear and its sources:
- Fear of abandonment _____

  _____

- Fear of disapproval _____

  _____

- Fear of rejection _____

  _____

- Fear of failures _____

  _____

- Fear of not receiving respect _____

  _____

- Others _____
- Identify your childish ways to cope with the above fear and vulnerabilities (e.g., internalization, silent treatment, pouting, running away, procrastination, controlling, temper outburst, passive aggressiveness, and avoidance). Do you need to seek forgiveness from your spouse regarding your past childish behaviors or lack of emotional self-sufficiency? Increase your emotional courage by learning to speak up and stand up for yourself. Accept and embrace emotional vulnerability, which is

very much human. Practice naming and labeling your fear and emotional needs to your spouse.

_____

_____

_____

_____

- Name your fear before God. Access and believe in God's promises to manage your vulnerability (1Chronicles 4:10; Jeremiah 29: 11-13).

_____

_____

_____

_____

- Externalize your vulnerability to a trusted member of your community. (e.g., pastor, a trusted male friend, a trusted male colleague, a professional counselor)

_____

- Choose a physical activity, a sport, or an exercise and practice it to clear your mind and release endorphins.

_____

- Find out your God-sent identity by working on your own D.A.T.A. (Desire, Abilities, Temperment, Asset):
  D – Your desires, your dreams, and the things you want to do and accomplish.

_____

_____

_____

A – Your strengths, your gifts, your talents, your upsides, your downsides, your weaknesses, and your liabilities.

_____

_____

_____

T – Your personality and temperament. Are you people oriented or task oriented? Are you an extrovert or an introvert?

_____

_____

_____

A – Your asset and your niche. What sets you apart from others?

I am a class of my own when it comes to: _____

He is one of a kind when it comes to: _____

You are so unique when it comes to: _____

_____

- Ask your spouse and two trusted friends to fill out a D.A.T.A. for you and compare findings to seek affirmation of your God-sent identity.
- Seek out a Christian psychologist/counselor to better manage your vulnerability and struggles with pornography.

STRATEGY #2

(For married men only)

TURN YOUR EYES UPON YOUR WIFE

"Drink waters out of your own cistern (of a pure marriage relationship), and fresh running waters out of your own well.... Let your fountain (of human life) be blessed (with the rewards of fidelity), and rejoice in the wife of your youth. Let her be as the loving hind and pleasant doe (tender, gentle, attractive) – let her bosom satisfy you at all times, and always be transported with delight in her love. Why should you, my son, be infatuated with a loose woman, embrace the bosom of an outsider, and go astray."

(Proverbs 5: 15, 18-20, the Amplified Bible)

- Value and increase couple time with your wife. A healthy

home is a couple-centered home. A kid-centered or an activity-centered home is not a healthy home.

- Value sex with your wife as a celebration of your ultimate love toward her. Your job is to satisfy her. Your own satisfaction is a bonus.

- Educate yourself and communicate with your wife about her woman's health cycle (e.g., peri-menopause, menopause) and adjust your sexual expectation accordingly and respectfully.

- Value your wife as God's special, custom-made, and unique gift and creation for you. She is the most suitable woman for you socially, emotionally, physically, and spiritually. (Your wife also has the responsibility to develop herself to be the right woman and the most suitable woman for you).

- Communicate to your wife of her God-sent values, which is the essence of emotional connection. (Studies have shown that marriage benefits men's health more than women, and the health benefits of marriage are related more to the social/emotional support provided by the spouse. The good news is that married men generally get health-enhancing social/emotional support from their spouse. The not-so-good news is married men don't do as good a job supplementing the support they get at home).

- Understand that the foundation of sexual intimacy, which is the ultimate intimacy between husband and wife, is based on other intimacies – recreational intimacy, creative intimacy, emotional intimacy, crisis intimacy, communication intimacy, and spiritual intimacy. Pursue these other intimacies for a strong foundation of sexual intimacy.

- Be thankful that God has provided you with the most suitable woman on earth. Genesis 2:18.

- Identify and strengthen your God-sent identity. One of the greatest gifts you can give to your wife is a unique and unshakeable sense of self.

RE-WIRE HOMEWORK

- Make it a habit to communicate to your wife verbally or by writing of her God-sent values (e.g., on the Mother's Day card you are going to give her, write something like the following: "Dear _____, I love you. You are a wonderful gift from God. Thank you for your love and support for our children and me. I thank God for putting you in my life. Love you always, Your Hubby." And do the same for her birthday card, anniversary card, Valentines Day card, etc.).
- During sex, keep your eyes open, keep some lights on, and nurture connection by saying "you satisfy me so much." Re-wire your brain with your wife's three dimensional images and sounds.
- Take your wife out for Couple Times (where, when, how, what).

_____

_____

- In your Pray without Ceasing, give thanks to God for your wife. You can pray the following: "Dear Lord, thank you for giving me _____ as my wife and lover. God, teach me to love and respect her more, to focus my eyes on her more. Lord, she is your gift for me. She is my healthy basket. I have to learn to accept her and appreciate her. Lord, make me the right person for her. Examine my heart and speak to me Lord. In Jesus' name, Amen."
- Make a habit to pray with your wife privately on a regular basis. How about starting this habit today?

STRATEGY #3

(For teenagers, single men, and men who are single again)

RENEW YOUR MIND ON WOMEN AS GOD'S CREATION

"Do not be conformed to this world (this age), (fashioned after and adapted to its external, superficial customs), but be transformed (changed) by the (entire) renewal of your mind (by its new ideals and its new attitude), so that you may prove (for yourselves) what is the good and acceptable and perfect will of God, even the thing which is good and acceptable and perfect (in His sight for you)."
(Romans 12:2, the Amplified Bible)

- Persistently and consistently practice the De-File and De-Cycle Pure at Heart strategies: put sexual objects "under the ban," neutralize the power of viewing women as sexual objects, and create major road blocks to short-circuit accessibility to using the addictive cycle to relieve pain.
- Mentally in your mind create the following new files and pictures about "Women as God's Creation."

The following information on woman characters is taken from Ed Silvoso's book, *Women: God's Secret Weapon:*

1. Women have not been mere privates in God's army; instead, they have been entrusted as key players in God's plan and strategy against Satan.
2. Mary was Jesus' first protector and first teacher.
3. Priscilla was more than a cookie maker. Together with Aquila, she taught Apollos (Acts 18:14, 25).
4. Lydia was the first European convert, and hers was the first household to be baptized (see Acts 16:14, 15).
5. Jesus' last earthly concern was for a woman, His mother (John 19:26, 27).
6. Women have an extraordinary sensitivity to

spiritual things. Jesus told Martha that He is the resurrection and the life (John 11: 25-27), and He told the Samaritan woman that He is the living water (see John 4). These women were in a state of confusion when Jesus found them, but both were able to hear, understand and believe profound truths. Think for a moment of the millions of people in the last 2,000 years whose lives have been transformed by these truths.

7. Mary Magdalene was the woman who saw the urgency and spent everything of value she had to comfort Jesus.

8. Women courageously risked their lives on Resurrection morning by visiting the tomb of a convicted criminal whose body was under 24-hour military guard.

9. When God spoke, Deborah had no doubt that God could deliver the Israelites from Sisera's army. See Judges.

It is true that while women are capable of stirring the noblest feelings in the male heart, they can also cause the deepest hurts. God has given women an attractive body, but women are not sexual objects in God's creation, women are key players in God's kingdom. For women in the church, they are God's daughters and sisters in Christ. In general, there are no fathers who want to harm their daughters and no brothers who want to harm their sisters (1Timothy 5:1-2). It is a woman's inner beauty that matters, not her external image. Read Proverbs 31: 10-31; Charm and grace are deceptive, and beauty is vain (because it is not lasting), but a woman who reverently and worshipfully fears the Lord, she shall be praised. Proverbs 31:30, the Amplified Bible.

- Examine your environment in downtime management: keep yourself away from the sources of ungodliness by staying busy and occupied with healthy activities and people.
- Have an accountability partner. Call him up when you are vulnerable with sexual temptation.
- Install or download an accountability program in your computer so that your Internet activities are transparent to your friends and accountability partners.
- Remember Christ died for every drop of your beta-endorphins and corticosteroids on the cross. Be a disciplined resource manager for your Creator and His intelligent design. Respect and value your own body by treating the biochemical resources in your body as precious commodity. Commit yourself to use and release these resources to enhance health within God's intelligent design, that is, with the woman you love and respect only on the marriage bed in the future.
- Nocturnal emissions or wet dreams are normal development during teenage years. A wet dream is just the body's way of getting rid of the extra fluid (semen) that has accumulated. It is not a deliberate way to misuse the biochemical resources in the body.

RE-WIRE HOMEWORK

- When you are tempted to see a woman as sexual object, rehearse to yourself the following: "She is a beautiful creation of God/she is God's daughter, my sister in Christ; she is not a sexual object. Christ died for her on the cross. She is a key player in God's kingdom." Proceed to use the neutralizing strategy
- List some healthy activities you can involve in to

in to help you stay away from sources of ungodliness, e.g., your Internet and TV at home.

_____

_____

_____

_____

- Pray the following prayer of thanksgiving: "Lord, thank
  you for all the natural feelings of sexual attraction you
  have created in me. I look forward to the day you bless
  me with the most suitable woman to fulfill my sexual
  needs. Amen."
- Ask God to give you an accountability partner to externalize your struggles and encourage one another.
- Select an accountability program to be installed in your
  computer.
- List some activities you can release your endorphins in a
  healthy way and within God's design (e.g., cardiovascular
  exercises)

_____

_____

_____

_____

CHAPTER FIVE

BRAIN ECONOMICS AND PORNOGRAPHY ADDICTION

THE NATURE OF PORNOGRAPHY ADDICTION

Pornography acts like a psychological, pain relief drug that allows a man to run away, effortless, to a fantasy world pre-determined by the pornography industry, to regain a sense of purpose, excitement, soothing comfort, acceptance, control and power, emotionally, physiologically, and neuro-chemically. In essence, pornography is not about sex.

Like any addiction, pornography addiction or frequent use of pornography is about running away from some sort of pain to seek emotional and chemical satisfaction in a fantasy world. Kids run away from pain. Adults face the pain with emotional self-sufficiency. Adults running away to pornography become men who are boys. They do so in isolation, self-centeredness, disconnection with loved ones, and in secrecy. Essentially the men are living a double life.

PORNOGRAPHY AND CHEMICAL SATISFACTION IN THE BRAIN

Sexual arousal in a pornography-affected brain increases the levels of:

- Endorphin – the natural Prozac, eases physical and emotional pain, helps make emotional pain bearable, creates attachment bonds, and triggers feelings of intense pleasure and joyful excitement.
- Oxytocin – the "love, cuddle, and attachment" hormones.
- Dopamine – the "feel-good" chemicals, enhances novelty and curiosity seeking, increases desire, wanting, craving, and mere pleasure seeking.

Healthy sex between husband and wife on the marriage bed also enjoys the same chemical satisfaction in the brain as a tremendous blessing from God within the Creator's design.

PORNOGRAPHY AND BRAIN ECONOMICS

Our brain is one of God's biggest intelligent designs in His creation. In order to help us live a healthy and godly life, our Creator put in checks and balances in the brain circuitry and functions. In general, the pre-frontal cortex, the CEO of our brain that governs and watches over our beliefs, values, and decision makings, put the brakes on the amygdala and the mid-brain, the fear center and the "wild beast" within, the instinctual and basal brain that plays a key role in activating the endorphin and dopamine reward system to crave for relief when certain cues and signals in our environment suggest imminent pleasure, excitement, escape, and soothing comfort.

In a pornography-affected brain, the checks and balances are off. Figuratively speaking, the mid-brain is 300 watt and the pre-frontal cortex is only 60 watt. A 60 watt pre-frontal cortex does not have enough power to convince a person and his mid-brain to stop craving for escape and soothing comfort by looking at pornography and women as sexual objects. That explains why good people do bad things, and Christian men go to pornography, know it is wrong, and cannot stop. It is like a conditional reflex - identical to the one that caused Russian psychologist Ivan Pavlov's famed dog to salivate at the ringing of the bell after it learned to associate the sound with food – that unleashes a craving for the soothing comfort associated with the maternal meaning of women's breasts and cleavages, the restoration of control and power associated with masturbation, and the total acceptance and chemical satisfaction associated with running away to the fantasy world of pornography. Pornography and sexual addiction is a serious health matter affecting men because it compromises the healthy checks and balances of the brain circuitry and functions.

OVERCOMING
PORNOGRAPHY ADDICTION

Pornography addiction is treatable. The very first step is to take up the responsibility to honor God's creation and intelligent design by resetting brain economics, restoring the checks and balances, and initiating healing. It gives the pre-frontal cortex a fighting chance against the amygdala, the fear center, and allows the brain's cognitive power to put a brake on the mid-brain, the "wild beast" within. What has to happen for that environmental cue (e.g., the soothing comfort associated with a woman's breasts and cleavage) to extinguish is not for the amygdala and mid-brain to become weaker but for the pre-frontal cortex, the brain of the higher purpose, to become stronger.

The De-file, De-Cycle, and Re-Wire Pure at Heart tools are all designed to give the pre-frontal cortex a fighting chance to be stronger and to increase its power and wattage to put the brakes on the mid-brain. The outcome is a gradual re-engaging of proper decision making and executive power in the mind to seek healthy choices and resources to live a healthy and godly life.

Ninety days is just about how long it takes for the brain to reset and shake off the immediate influence of pornography, the non-substance drug in sexual addiction. To begin with, practice the Pure at Heart tools, especially the tool of neutralizing and under the ban, for a minimum of 90 days. After 90 days, turn the Pure at Heart tools into a life time practice until the day we meet our Creator.

CHAPTER SIX

SHAME AND PORNOGRAPHY ADDICTION

Good day, Sir. I am 19 years old, from the Philippines, I thank God for unexpectedly pointing me to your book, and it is a life changing book. I am on a double life for a very long time. Because of your book, it made turn exactly 180 degree away from sexual immorality and pointed me towards God. By now, I am still practicing the De-file, De-cycle and Re-wire approach. The book clears out all the demonizing rationalization that I have been telling to myself after getting back to the real world. By reminding me of who's the real enemy, I finally caught myself being used by Satan who is killing my spiritual life gradually. It helps a lot when you put some scientific ideas behind the situation that I have undergone; it explained to me the bio-chemicals that have been working inside me. Pure at Heart makes me understand that I am suffering on an internal pain, and I want myself to get out of it by using my natural painkillers. I have been asking God for answers, and failing God for the nth time, then, I read that I am on the addictive cycle. I don't want to be the same again; this book rescued me from the fires of lusts of flesh, I am now reclaiming my path to righteousness and to godliness. Sir, again,

thank you very much for being an instrument of God to save me.
God is my hero and you are his sword...

The internal pain experienced by the above mentioned young man is the pain of shame. There is no emotional pain in this world that is heavier and more severe than the pain of shame. According to Merle A. Fossum and Marilyn J. Mason, authors of *Facing Shame: Families in Recovery*, shame is an inner sense of being inadequate, not good enough, not measured up, and unworthy as a human being. It is the ongoing premise that "there is something wrong with me as a person." Guilt is the developmentally more mature, though painful feeling of regret one has about behaviour that has violated a personal value. Guilt does not reflect directly upon one's identity nor diminish one's sense of personal worth.

In essence, shame is about the person, guilt is about the behaviour. None of us is immune from shame because we don't have perfect parents, perfect family upbringing, perfect teachers, and perfect schools. Some of us are much more affected by shame more often than others especially when there are abuses and addiction in the person's family history. Addiction and shame are inseparable. We cannot treat pornography addiction without treating the shame problem.

Unfortunately many of us are not aware that we re carrying a huge load of baggage called shame. All we can do is to wear a mask to cover the shame (e.g., to become an extreme caregiver to seek approval and affirmation) or to run away to some unhealthy places (e.g., the pornography world) to seek soothing comfort and control to relieve the pain of shame.

In their book *Facing Shame*, Fossum and Mason outlined the following characteristics and masks of a shame-based family and relationship:

- **Excessive control**. You cannot be yourself. You live or family and relationship:

- **Excessive control**. You cannot be yourself. You live or work with rigidity of values. There is little freedom to interpret the gray areas of life experience in an individual or creative way. Anything unique to oneself or creative is more vulnerable and avoided.
- **Perfection**. You are feeling you are never good enough, or something is wrong with you.
- **Blame**. If something doesn't happen as you planned, blame the person (yourself or someone else).
- **Denial**. Deny feelings especially the negative and vulnerable ones like anxiety, fear, loneliness, grief, rejection, neediness, and caring.
- **Unreliability**. Relationships remaining at the immature level, individuals are repeatedly disappearing on their emotional connections. You cannot count on each other to provide emotional connection in a consistent manner.
- **Incompleteness**. Disagreements to go unresolved for years. People in the family are unaware that they leave so much unresolved; when it is brought to their attention they may not know how to resolve or compete a transaction.
- **No talk**. The no-talk rule, don't talk about disrespectful, shameful, and abusive behaviour. Don't talk about grief or family secrets. This hallmark of shame is a huge barrier to intimacy.
- **Disqualification**. When disrespectful, shameful, abusive or addictive behaviour occurs, use disqualification and denial to reframe or disguise it, e.g., "When your father is not drunk, he is a good man." "Your father beat you up because he is under a lot of stress with the family finances."

THE DIFFERENT MASKS OF
A SHAME-BASED FAMILY
AND RELATIONSHIP

- **The fairytale family/the fairytale Christian family**. Family members look good to all outsiders. The persons inside have disappeared, the outside self is all that is known. They know what car to drive, what clothing to wear, what meals and wine to serve, what books to read, what vacation spots to choose, what churches to attend. They cannot let anyone know how inadequate they feel. No one is allowed to tell others outside the family how empty and lonely the family members feel.

- **The disconnected, emotionally cut-off family**. Family members have turned away from one another in order to cope with the pain of shame. Some families go so far as to abandon all rituals and special occasions, e.g., birthdays, Christmas get together. Brothers and sisters in adulthood may go for months or years never validating their relationship by communicating anything real about their lives. The have ceased to engage in emotional dialogue.

- **The rough and tough family**. Highly stereotypic gender role, with the macho male and the culturally stereotyped passive female. The language of toughness is spoken here, "Get your butt out of that chair and let your mother sit down." The family script is "life is tough; we'll survive it." It is not alright to be sad, lonely, needing, or tender in this family.

- **The nice-nice family**. "If you love me, you will never be in conflict with me." Interpersonal language is quite persuasive and always indirect, such as, "you know, Jessica's mother told me that Jessica goes to church every week."

The manipulation is covert; requests are seldom direct. Anger cannot be expressed openly. Individuals from these nice-nice families fear conflict and accommodate others out of their blind loyalty to their families. Children often are quite confused because the parents "heap" their love on them by controlling them.

God does not want us to develop a shame-based identity out of a shame-bound family and relationship system. A God-sent identity is a respect-based identity showered by God-worth in a respect-bound relationship system.

HALLMARKS OF A RESPECT-BOUND FAMILY AND RELATIONSHIP

- **Every person is different**. Every person is created differently and valued by God.
- **Individuals take in life experiences, make mistakes, and learn from them**. They are free to continue to learn and grow. They didn't start out assuming perfection and they continue to live in the insecurity of not having a claim to perfect their doing. Making peace with that insecurity or at least accommodating to it carries the benefit that people can continue to learn.
- **It is not possible in a close relationship with a person and never hurt that person**. We all have weaknesses, blind spots and our dark sides. Misunderstandings are part of the process of relationships. They are regarded as a problem to be dealt with and are resolved as part of the ongoing dialogue. This does not mean that the dialogue is never intense or angry. True relationship dialogue, the "basement" talk and the elevator tool mentioned with the

re-wire homework in Chapter Four, includes those feelings "from the gut." What it means is a mutual commit-
ment to take in and respond honestly without threats to
break off the exchange or the relationship.

- **Intimate relationships involve antagonism and hostili-
ty as well as loving**. Intimate relationships provide more
occasions for conflict, and conflict between intimates is
usually more intense.

- **A respectful system has more variety and resilience in
interpreting life experiences because the flow of life
events will be perceived more on their own merits than
as a judgment of the person**. The losses are no less painful, the changes no less forceful. But it has greater capaci-
ty to absorb more of the stresses of change and still retain
its integrity (Luke 6: 46-49, the Amplified Bible).

- **Individuals are increasing in awareness of what it is to
be a person**. They have an increasing knowledge and respect for the dilemmas, pains and surprises of being human. They learn to trust life. "I used to plan my life and
now I just show up!" is an expression that someone has
come to terms with trusting his/her life given by God.

Our shame does not come from Jesus. When Jesus first saw
us in our mother's womb, He has already fallen in love with
us, and we are God's precious sons and daughters. We are so
valuable and important to Jesus that He gave His life for us on
the cross. Jesus is proud of us as a person; He is not ashamed of
us. He has a plan for you and me. His yoke is useful, good, not
harsh, and His burden is light and easy to be borne (Matthew
11: 28-30, the Amplified Bible).

The first step to let go of shame is to name the shame .The
task of naming (Genesis 2: 18-25, the Amplified Bible) has
a powerful healing effect so that we know who we are and
what we are facing. We need to name the baggage tag before

we know which baggage to let go. Once we name the shame, we can face it by releasing the shame to Jesus and He would nail the shame on the cross and disconnect its power. We can now face the shame and the pain, neither by running away from it nor by putting a mask over it, but by practicing the lifetime Pure at Heart tools and claiming the brand new God-sent baggage as our own, which is His wholesome plan and purpose and God-sent identity for you and me.

CHAPTER SEVEN

RE-CLAIM
YOUR PATHWAY
TO GODLINESS

*One of our missionaries in Cote d'Ivoire way back in the seventies,
I think, Walter Olsen, led an old Baoule (bow-li) man to Christ.
He tried to start him out with some teaching and left him with the
church in his village. The next time he was in that village the old
man was there and was still very excited about Jesus. When the
missionary, Walter Olsen, asked him how he was doing, he said,
"Jesus is wonderful! He is more wonderful than the breasts of a
young maiden!" That wraps up a lot for me. When we understand
the beauty of Jesus, the ugly twist that the world has put on the
beautiful female body is straightened out. Jesus is more wonderful
than the biggest distraction that many men face, that of a twisted
appreciation for one of God's best gifts!*

Tim Tjosvold, Canadian Missionary in Africa

ACCESSING THE POWER OF THE DOCTOR WITHIN

- **Practice God's presence by praying without ceasing (1 Thessalonians 5:17).** There is a Doctor, Jehovah Rophe, living within each one of us, and that is God in the Person of the Holy Spirit. When we come to know Christ as our personal Saviour, God gives us a new engine, a new creation. The Holy Spirit, the Doctor Within, also moves in to live with us. The Doctor Within wants us to pick up a new key and start a new engine and use the new engine. The new engine is much smoother, it is quieter, it is much more efficient, it lasts and endures longer, and it has the right power. But the old engine—our old self—also wants us to take the old key and start the old engine again, and to make noises. When we keep in touch with the Doctor Within through prayer without ceasing and reading His Words, we access the power of the new engine.

- **Practice God's presence by accessing a community of safe people/men.** Healing does not happen in isolation. Healing happens in a community of safe people. Satan's battle plan is to strike down the children of God, men and women, one person at a time, in isolation. Satan knows men use less of God's community to externalize their vulnerability, and it is relatively easier for Satan to keep men under his bondage. Men's ministry is one of the most important ministries within God's community, and yet many churches and their leaders have placed less priority on strengthening men's ministry. The Doctor Within, Jehovah Rophe, cares about our total health: physically, emotionally, socially, and spiritually. Make use of the community of Godly men around you. Connect with the men in your faith community in a group setting or in one-on-one relationships. Healthy men mean healthy homes, healthy marriages, and healthy communities.

- **Surrender everything to God, through and through (Romans12: 1).** Do not keep your "basement or closets" locked from God's entry. Nothing withheld. Nothing off limits. No parts of our lives from birth to death. No parts of our beings from conscious to unconscious. No parts of our minds. No parts of our emotions. (From Beth Moore's book, *When Godly People Do Ungodly Things*). Stop holding too tightly onto your money, possessions, children, spouse, church, ministry, or career. Everything we have belongs to God. When we hold onto things too tightly, they belong to us, not God, and we begin to manage our possessions our way, not God's way.

- **Take a cue from the Roman philosopher Seneca** who advised that we count each day as a separate life. This present moment is precious. It is the only moment in which we have any power.

- **Be thankful and actively give thanks (1 Thessalonians 5: 18).** Ongoing and chronic feelings of dissatisfaction are yellow and red flags that need to be well inspected. Otherwise, vulnerability will grow. Such feelings may mean something vital is missing and we need to seek God and other's counsel without delay.

- **Practice the 3-step De-file, De-Cycle, Re-Wire Pure at Heart approach persistently and consistently.** The power of deliverance from the Doctor Within is channeled through the process of De-filing, De-cycling and Re-wiring.

- **Pray God's Word – the best weapon to fight and defeat Satan's battle plan (based on Beth Moore's book, *Praying God's Word*).**

PRAYING GOD'S WORD

For though we walk (live) in the flesh, we are not carrying on our warfare according to the flesh and using mere human weapons. For the weapons of our warfare are not physical (weapons of flesh and blood), but they are mighty before God for the overflow and destruction of strongholds. (Inasmuch as we) refute arguments and theories and reasoning and every proud and lofty thing that sets itself up against the (true) knowledge of God; and we lead every thought and purpose away captive into the obedience of Christ (the Messiah, the Anointed One). (2 Corinthians 10:3-5, Amplified Bible).

IN OUR BATTLE AGAINST SATAN, PRAYING GOD'S WORD KEEPS OUR MIND CAPTIVE TO CHRIST INSTEAD OF OUR OWN PAIN AND VULNERABILITY.

On putting images of sexual objects under the ban

- Lord God, Your Word says that You bless the home of the righteous but Your curse is on the house of the wicked. (Proverbs. 3:33). Lord, please help me cleanse my home and put under the ban any kind of materials that support or fuel sexual wickedness. Make this the kind of home You can fully bless.

On the power of neutralizing

- Lord, help me to neutralize the power of sexual lust and temptation and keep my eyes looking straight ahead and my gaze fixed directly before me. Make level paths for my feet and strengthen me to take only the ways that are firm. Help me not to swerve to the right or the left; keep my feet from evil. (Proverbs. 4:25-27).

On stopping the use of our god-given natural pain killer (endorphins and corticosteroids) outside of god's intelligent design

- Lord, I renounce all these uses of natural pain killers in my body as an instrument of unrighteousness, and by so doing I ask You to break all bondages that Satan has brought into my life through that involvement. I confess my participation. I confess that I am responsible for giving Satan a foothold in my life, and I renounce the involvement with him through my God-given neurochemistry in my body. I now present my body to You as a living sacrifice, holy and acceptable to You, and I reserve the sexual use of my body only on the marriage bed. (Romans 12:1).

- Lord, I want a set of clean hands and a pure heart, and I don't want dishonesty and a double life. Lord, I renounce the use of masturbation as a way to release my natural pain killers that restore comfort and control outside of God's will. Every time I am tempted to masturbate, remind me that Christ died for every drop of the precious natural pain killers in my body. My body is the very sanctuary of the Holy Spirit, and I want to manage my body by clean hands. (Psalm 24: 3-5).

On stopping the use of pornography as a form of medication to soothe our vulnerabilities (insecurity, fear, rejection, failures, etc.). Go to God and His community instead.

- I am seeking you, Lord, and You will answer me, You will deliver me from all my fears. (Psalm 34:4).

- Lord God, I desire to claim the words Moses delivered to Your ancient people: Help me not to be afraid. Enable me to stand firm so I will see the deliverance that You, the Lord, will bring me today. You, Lord, will fight for me;

help me only to be still. (Exodus 14:13-14).

- Father God, make me strong and courageous. Help me not to be afraid or terrified because of anyone else, for You, the Lord my God, go with me; You will never leave me or forsake me. (Deuteronomy 31:6).
- Father, teach me and help me to cast all my anxiety on You because You care for me. (I Peter 5:7).
- Lord, my God, may Your unfailing love be my comfort, according to Your promise to Your servant. (Psalm 119:76).
- Father, according to Your word, it is better not to eat meat or drink wine or to do anything else that will cause a brother or sister to fall. (Romans 14:21). I pray that not only will I be mindful of this exhortation with others but You will cause those around me not to do things that will cause me to fall! Lord, I understand healing does not happen in isolation. Healing happens in a community of safe people. Lord, help me and convict me to connect with a community of Godly men.

On focusing on my wife, the gift from God

- Lord Jesus, help me to focus on my wife and her whole person. Open my eyes to whatever is true about my wife, whatever is noble, whatever is right, whatever is pure, whatever is lovely, whatever is admirable – if anything is excellent or praiseworthy – help me think about such things about my wife. (Philippians 4:8-9).

AFFAIR-PROOF YOUR MARRIAGE

THREE TYPES OF AFFAIRS:

- The one-night stand
- The entangled affair – "fatal attraction"
- Sexual addiction – addiction to affairs

The entangled affair is the most problematic and common form of adultery, and one of the most stubborn to rehabilitate due to extensive emotional involvement. The man and woman have a relationship – often akin to the marriage relationship. The similarity to the marriage bond is part of the reason it's so dangerous: the man is finding needs met that he has been seeking to have met in his marriage for years, usually unsuccessfully.

From Dave Carder's *Torn Asunder*

In a recent issue of *Physician,* a magazine published by Focus on the Family, a medical doctor shared the following reflection on his affair with a young woman in his office:

"Medicine is an entity of intense moments and emotions. Men and women who care for the sick and dying often forge special bonds as they share experience of pain, tragedy, anger, frustration and, yes, joy. From my own life and practice, I know that in the middle of the sorrow and trouble in patients' lives and the difficulty I face attempting to practice, I sometimes look to the nurses with who I work for some normalcy, just as they look to me. We want to see a smiling face, hear a joke and experience something that pulls us temporarily out of the blood and the breathlessness; the drunkenness and the stupidity that often accompany our work. We depend on one another throughout the day until we can go home to the ones we love. A potential stumbling block in this arrangement is that, like many physicians, I work with some lovely women. Bright and professional, some of them have a manner of speech, a favorite perfume, and a tilt of laughter or a curve of body that makes them appealing. This attraction creates a dangerous environment in which powerful feelings and physical exhaustion may lead men and women to seek comfort in the wrong direction – ultimately turning them into adulterers… All of those factors converged so that I committed adultery with a young woman in my office. She understood the enormous pressures of my medical career, and I thought that she could untangle the mess of emotions I was struggling to unravel. I believed she was an escape that I deserved. I convinced myself that I was rescuing her from a miserable life as well. I bought into the deception that I had found the "right" person at last, and that all was well when we were together."

The experience of the medical doctor speaks truly to the pathology of affair and its destructive process. An affair does not happen out of the blue; it evolves in a very predictable pattern. An affair usually begins when a person is unaware of or ignores his/her vulnerability, and at the same time does not practice proper boundaries in relationships. When a person is vulnerable, his/her mind, body, and spirit are looking for pain relief. The affair process further evolves when the pain relief comes from a person of the opposite sex who is not the spouse, and that person acts like a high-performing, addictive drug who provides a sense of comfort, a listening ear, validation, affirmation, emotional attachment, escape and rescue. The affair is consummated when sexual intercourse is involved, and the addiction to one another turns into high gear. The affair continues and sustains itself by mutual rationalization of love and the two parties needing one another. An affair is not about true love; it is about an unhealthy, addictive relationship and experience. As one woman put it, when she got caught again by her husband, she felt like she was an alcoholic addicted to booze, except her liquor was the youth pastor she had an affair with.

THE PATHOLOGY OF AN AFFAIR: A FOUR-STEP DESTRUCTIVE PROCESS

1. VULNERABILITY

Vulnerability means there is added risk, not added value, in a person's life. Vulnerability often occurs when a person is:

- under a lot of stress
- grieving major losses
- feeling insecure and looking for affirmation and respect
- feeling rejected and looking for validation
- going through a burnout
- experiencing boredom and looking for fun and excitement
- not aware of his/her personal weaknesses, e.g., boundary issues with persons of the opposite sex, e.g., often wanting to save or rescue someone
- having unfulfilled expectations and unexpressed needs in the marriage

In his book *Torn Asunder*, Dave Carder writes:

"When we are vulnerable, we are emotionally run down, our defenses are down, our perspective on things is clouded, we are not able to make judgment based on truth, and everything is seen through an emotional filter. Pain is intensified. Therefore, the pursuit of relief from pain is also intensified. When you are vulnerable, a situation that might otherwise be safe may now be unsafe."

2. Emotional, Non-Physical Involvement

In the pathology of an affair, the gray area is where much game playing occurs. Don't worry, we're just friends. Don't worry, we're just doing ministry together. He has never touched me. We are not doing anything wrong. Because people tend to say that nothing is going on when there is no physical contact, they feel safe because they think they are still walking within boundaries. In reality, they are really crossing the line. This innocent "playing around" can lead to the next destructive step in the process: physical contact.

Emotional involvement and violation of boundaries occur when a man and a woman who are not married to one another:

- share intimate information about their past
- share intimate information about personal struggles
- share intimate information about marital problems
- want to support, rescue, and protection for their wounded souls

The following story from a woman illustrates the danger of emotional involvement:

"Ralph and I became friends after meeting at work. We began consoling each other over each of our failing marriages. Put it this way, because we were leaning on each other for support, things '

between me and Ralph ended up getting heavy ... maybe four or five times we got into some pretty heavy petting, you know, touchy feely, and then intercourse on just one occasion."

Other warning signs when relationship boundaries are not well established:

(From Dr. Debbie L. Cherry, Focus on the Family Canada, May 2008)

- Do your conversations with your friend include things that should be kept between you and your spouse?
- Do you find yourself daydreaming about your friend?
- Have you found yourself withdrawing from your spouse emotionally or physically?
- Do you look for excuses to see or talk to your friend?
- Do you share thoughts, feelings and problems with your friend instead of your spouse?
- Are you convinced that your friend understands you better than your spouse?
- Is there flirting or sexual tension?
- Do you look for "legal" ways to touch your friend (brush lint off his jacket, help her with her coat)?
- Do you find yourself paying attention to how you look before you see your friend?
- Is there any secrecy about your relationship (how much time you spend together, what you do together, what you talk about)?

3. Physical Involvement

Once an affair gets physical, it is hard to get out. It is like a full-blown addiction to the relationship.

4. Rationalizations for Continuing the Affair and reasoning against guilt

- "Just one more time."

- "If my wife only met my needs, I wouldn't do this."
- "I understand her so much better than her husband does."
- "She needs me."
- "We work well together."
- "It won't happen again."
- "I'm just too weak."
- "If only God would give me the strength to stop."
- "God knows that I need this."
- "King David did it; it can't be that bad."
- "No one else knows, so what's the harm?"
- "God will forgive us."
- "There are worse sins."
- "God loves us no matter what we do."

HOW TO AFFAIR-PROOF YOUR MARRIAGE

SET AND MAINTAIN APPROPRIATE BOUNDARIES WITH PERSONS OF THE OPPOSITE SEX WHO ARE NOT YOUR SPOUSE.

- Do not disclose and share intimate information and personal struggles with a person who is not your spouse on a one-on-one basis. If someone of the opposite sex bares his/her soul with you, encourage the person to seek professional help. Do not play the rescuer role, otherwise you cross boundaries.
- When you meet with a person of the opposite sex in your office, if possible, keep your office door fully or half opened. If possible, construct or choose offices with a glass window in order to create some transparency for the actions within the office.
- When you travel with co-workers on business trips, (e.g. a

conference), do not meet with someone of the opposite sex alone in your hotel room. Meet in the public or in a meeting room with people around.

- If possible, avoid visiting someone of the opposite sex alone in his or her home. This applies to the "Handy Man." You are handy and have the gift of helping others. A recently separated single parent needs some repair in her bathroom, and your spouse send you there to help. Bring your spouse or kids with you. Do not create a situation where you are alone with someone who is potentially vulnerable.

SEEK HEALTHY WAYS TO RELIEVE PAIN

- Identify your pain (fear, insecurity, rejection, betrayal, failure, feeling not good enough, getting no respect in the marriage, etc.)
- Do not internalize your pain, externalize it. Share your pain with your spouse, and/or with someone of the same gender whom you trust. (This is a difficult practice for men because they are supposed to have answers and solutions. It has taken me a long time to willingly share my own insecurities with my wife). If necessary, seek professional counseling yourself.
- Decrease vulnerability by practicing healthy self-care. Exercise regularly. Practice good communication with your spouse and children. Remember: Your life is bigger than your work. Self-care is not equal to selfishness.

AFFAIR RECOVERY: REPAIRING THE BROKEN ATTACHMENT BOND AND FORGIVING INJURIES

"After I cried and screamed, I went to the bathroom and threw up."
Elizabeth Edwards on living with the infidelity of John
Edwards, her husband and former U.S. Democratic
presidential candidate

Affair is a severe, and sometimes fatal, relationship injury. Affair critically injures the attachment bond between husband and wife. The following steps are necessary to repair and rebuild the broken relationship:

EXTERNALIZING THE PAIN AND THE LOSS

The injured partner speaks directly to the traumatic nature of the relationship injuries, such as, loss, rejection, betrayal, and abandonment.

VALIDATING THE PAIN AND ACCEPTING CONSEQUENCES

The injuring partner acknowledges the wounded partner's pain, takes ownership of the damages and responsibility for the justified consequences, and expresses regret, remorse, and shame.

RESTORING TRUST AND SETTING BOUNDARY

Discloses all facts about the affair; implement strict boundary; treats the other person in the affair like an addicted drug, and stops going there for self soothing and emotional satisfaction.

PRACTICING HEALTHY SELF CARE

The injured partner decreases isolation and secrecy. Seeks support and discloses hurt and loss to someone who is trustworthy. Seeks professional help if necessary.

MAKING A CHOICE AND A DECISION

Choose a rescue mission or a salvaging mission for the marriage. A rescue mission believes there are survivors; a salvaging mission brings out the body bags.

Make a decision to accept apology and initiate forgiveness.

You can let the affair hurt you, but don't let it ruin you. No decision, no learning. No action, no learning.

IDENTIFYING THE UNHEALTHY PROCESS OF ADDICTION IN THE AFFAIR

Affair is more than a marital issue. It is an emotional health issue.

There is no healthy alcoholic, healthy drug addict, healthy pornography addict, healthy workaholic, healthy control freak/behavioral addict, and healthy gambling addict. There is also no healthy adulterer.

A healthy marriage begins with a healthy partner. Seek professional help if necessary.

CREATING A SAFETY PLAN

The injured partner needs to feel safe and reassurance that the injury will not happen again.

Develop and implement a plan designed to restore trust and safety in the relationship.

RESTORING EMOTIONAL HEALTH AND CONNECTION IN MARRIAGE

Rebuilding the marriage after the affair is a shared responsibility between husband and wife. Seek couple therapy if necessary.

MANAGING PAIN AND EXPECTATIONS

Rehabilitating a severe injury requires time, hard work, and consistent effort.

Injuries may be forgiven, but they never disappear. Severe injury usually comes with chronic pain. Emotional triggers are not uncommon.

Forgiveness is "day-by-day" for the couple. It is human and not abnormal for the injured spouse struggles to forgive the injuring partner. As Elizabeth Edwards shared in her new book, *Resilience*, about her struggle to forgive her husband of 31 years, "I am imperfect in a million ways, but I always thought I was… the kind of wife to whom a husband would be faithful."

Wise and timely professional counsel would help pave the way for a healthy recovery from relationship injury caused by infidelity.

CHAPTER NINE

CREATING A LEGACY OF PURITY IN THE FAMILY

I looked at pornography when I was a teenager. I am a guy, what do you expect? I talked to my youth pastor about pornography, and he had the same struggle as a man. I don't spend time looking at pornography now. It is a waste of my time; I have better things to do.

Testimony of a young Christian man

As you have found out in Chapter Two, pornography and viewing women as sexual objects is not about sex. Pornography is a medication used by some men to seek comfort and restore a sense of control by releasing their natural pain killers outside God's plan. The road to healthy and godly living is to stop putting eggs in the basket called pornography and create other healthy baskets to put your eggs in. Healthy baskets include connection to a community of safe people, externalization of your pains and fear to God, a spouse, or a man you trust, and regular physical exercise to release natural pain killers within God's will.

As fathers, we want our sons to pursue a life of purity. Just like exposure to other drugs such as alcohol, pot, and cigarettes, many teenagers, Christians or non-Christians, are exposed to pornography either on the Internet or through friends in school. The fact is that not every teenager carries his involvement with pornography into adulthood or continues to view women as sexual objects. Likewise, not every teenager who tries smoking in high school turns into an adult with nicotine addiction. What makes the difference? What made the above mentioned young Christian man decide to stop looking at pornography and spare himself from a lifetime of sexual addiction?

As parents, we need to realize that there is no guarantee that our sons will not turn to pornography in their adult lives to seek comfort and relieve pain. One thing we do have control over is creating a family environment that prevents seeds from being sown in our sons' minds and bodies that using impure ways to release natural painkillers to soothe their emotional ups and downs is okay. It isn't okay, and that message starts with us.

PURITY IN THE FAMILY BEGINS WITH YOU

Do the messages in the previous chapters speak to you directly? If so, you need to come before God and ask Him to restore you with clean hands and a pure heart. Go back to Chapter Six and pray God's Words to renounce your impure ways. You cannot expect your sons to pursue purity if you live a double life yourself. Consistently use the De-File, De-Cycle, and Re-Wire Pure at Heart tools to restore healthy and godly living. In addition, ask yourself the following questions, based on Harry Schaumburg's book, *False Intimacy*, to assess your emotional self-sufficiency:

- Is my primary goal with my sons to do everything I can to help them avoid failure and achieve success as they grow through adolescence and into adulthood?
- How emotionally detached from my sons am I? Do I focus too much on external issues?
- Am I able to move toward my sons' pain as they grapple with getting good grades in school, finding acceptance from friends, or trying to make the team? Or am I afraid that doing so will make me aware of my own fears and failures as a father?
- Do I deal with the agony I feel as I sense the agony my sons sometimes feel, or do I back away from my sons' agony because I can't face the pain within myself?
- Do I run away from the tough issues? Am I content simply to be the "good father" and meet my sons' material needs?
- Because I'm afraid of pain and disappointment, do I somehow put a sense of obligation on my sons, in which they feel that the only way they can be acceptable to me is to succumb to the pressure to succeed and make me feel good?
- Do I find myself giving so much to my work that I have little or nothing emotionally to give to my sons? Do I avoid intimacy?
- Do my sons feel free to really reveal to me what they are thinking and doing, without fear of rejection, ignorance, and/or judgment?
- Am I willing to trust God with my pain and disappointment, to allow Him to be the source of ultimate fulfillment in my life? Will I submit to Him all my desire and my needs for relationship?

If you answer "yes" to some of the above questions, please come before God and ask Him to show you healthy ways to grow as a man and to put away childish ways to deal with adult and parental matters. Practice the tools described in the Re-Wire Homework in Chapter Four.

CREATE AN ENVIRONMENT WHERE YOUR SONS CAN SHARE NEEDS AND DESIRES SAFELY

Emotional safety is the foundation of a trusting parent-child relationship. Your sons may not need advice on how to handle the situation; they may need comfort and support. Be willing to listen to the despair and disappointment. Otherwise your sons may turn to unhealthy ways to seek comfort. Remember, pornography is a comfort drug that offers soothing pain relief. A healthy dose of emotional safety at home created by one or both parents is an antidote to the sickness of seeking unhealthy ways for pain relief.

USE APPROPRIATE PHYSICAL AFFECTION

Many men reported "true" to #39 of the True/False self-assessment questions in Chapter Two: I grew up in a home where my mom and/or dad showed very little or restricted emotional connection and physical affection. Physical affection provides affirmation of love and acceptance as well as comfort and strengthening of the parent-child attachment bond. It is another antidote parents can provide for their sons to safeguard against unhealthy ways of seeking comfort and control. Research has suggested that children who have not received the attentive presence of the parent are at greater risk for seeking chemical satisfaction from external sources (e.g., drugs, pornography) later in life.

PUT YOUR HOME UNDER THE BAN OF ANY IMAGES THAT DEPICT WOMEN AS SEXUAL OBJECTS

Lord God, Your Word says that You bless the home of the righteous but Your curse is on the house of the wicked. (Proverbs. 3:33). Lord, please help me cleanse and put under the ban in my home any kind of materials that support or fuel sexual wickedness. Make this the kind of home You can fully bless.

Turn the above prayer in Chapter Six into practice and reduce the chance that your sons will be exposed to impure images and use them as a medication for pain relief. If possible, install blocking software on your home PC. Move the home computer screen so that all family members can view what is being accessed or worked on.

CONNECT YOUR SONS WITH A COMMUNITY OF HEALTHY FRIENDS

Start at an early age, and throughout their different stages of childhood and adolescence, intentionally connect your sons with a community of healthy peers in which they do not need to work hard to gain acceptance, support, and counsel. This loving community is another antidote to the sickness of seeking unhealthy ways of seeking comfort and escaping pain.

> "We are called by God to be God's and each other's companion. The term "companion" is rich in meaning, coming from the Latin com panis ("with bread"). We are called to deliver on the promise that we will share bread with others, that we will be one with each other. There are many names for this sharing: utopia, communities, and the kingdom of God. It is this sharing that Jesus calls us to. He does so in the sacramental feast known as the Lord's Supper. He breaks bread and shares it with us."
>
> From Michael Frost's *Exiles: Living Missionally in a Post-Christian Culture*

CHAPTER TEN

STAY EQUIPPED IN YOUR JOURNEY

Whenever an unclean memory file surfaces in your mind, ask God to permanently 'overwrite' that file with a beautiful, wholesome memory instead. I have practiced this, and have found it to be wonderfully effective. Although our bodies do not become more beautiful with age, I believe our minds ought to become more beautiful with age. There may be many memories of things that have marred or defiled a person's mind. When a person becomes mature enough to realize that the garden of their mind has been marred by memories that are impure, each time that person comes across such a memory in the defiled garden of their mind, they should ask God to replace it with something beautiful and good, step by step reclaiming the garden of their mind so that it becomes more beautiful as they age. The goal is a mind that is like a beautiful garden in the sight of God, where you and Him can fellowship together.

Kirk Durston, Campus Crusade for Christ

The calling to be a champion of purity is a lifelong battle and journey. The hyper-sexualized world we live in will not go away, journey. The hyper-sexualized world we live in will not go away, and pornography will stay as long as it is a profitable business. It is our responsibility to practice the tools of neutralizing and putting sexual images "under the ban" every day until the day we go to see our Creator. I neutralize everyday, in the YMCA when I do my workout, in the bank when I do my banking business, in the church when I greet people at the front entrance and when I worship in front of the worship team, in the restaurant when I dine with my wife, and on the streets in the summer time when I am driving in my neighborhood. I neutralize because I don't want to add another ungodly file in my mind. Adding another file will wake up all the other ungodly files stored up in my mind over the years. I cannot delete the old files, but I have a choice not to add another ungodly file. My responsibility is to "overwrite" my mind with the wonderful intimacy my wife and I share, the faithful provision and guidance my God has provided for my children and family, and the purpose and meaning God has directed me to pursue.

Neutralizing and putting sexual images "under the ban" are external Pure at Heart tools. We also need to pursue internal tools, the tools that equip us to be at peace with ourselves, to be proud of our God-worth, and to use our gifts and talents to live a simple, focused life and create eternal meanings in people's lives. Internal tools direct us to healthy sources to meet our need for intimacy, connection, emotional self-sufficiency, and a healthy identity.

Over the years, God has helped me to face my shame and to find and accept my own identity in His intelligent design. I have learned to speak up and stand up for myself, to let go of excessive control of my life and possessions, to be proud of my son who is very different from me, to love and respect my wife and her body, and most of all, to learn to trust God and master. You might benefit from seeking the advice and guidance of a reputable pastor, counselor, or psychologist to help you find peace within yourself.

At the time of writing of this last chapter of the book, I was sitting on my deck under the beautiful Alberta morning sun and reflected on the following prayer from John Piper's book, *Don't Waste Your Life*:

> *"O Father, grant your church to love your glory more than gold – to cease her love affair with comfort and security. Grant that we seek the Kingdom first and let the other things come as you will. Grant that we move toward need and not toward ease. Grant that the firm finality of our security in Christ free us to risk our homes and health and money on earth. Help us to see that if we try to guard our wealth, instead of using it to show it's not our god, then we will waste our lives, however we succeed. Amen."*

I trust that this will also be your personal prayer as you allow God to equip you with external and internal Pure at Heart tools that help you set the course for a lifelong journey of godly living in our sexualized world.

In closing, I want to share the following story of a young man's Pure at Heart journey:

> *"Hi Dr. Sheh, personally I am doing well. I still haven't masturbated once. The temptation has been there at times still but the Lord is helping me recognize the reasons why in the moment and giving me the ability to just pause and let the moment pass. My wife and I are well. Our relationship seems to be healing and we are enjoying each other's company. I am still neutralizing and continue to keep our house under the ban. I am finding that those tasks are becoming mundane to me. Not so much of a stretch anymore. And I am constantly trying to over-write the files in my mind as they pop up. Images of things I have seen continue to surface in my mind. I continue to pray for Jesus to remove them and replace them with wholesome images.*

surface in my mind. I continue to pray for Jesus to remove them and replace them with wholesome images.

The most amazing thing happened a while back. I had an image come into my mind and I prayed for the Lord to over-write it with a wholesome image and when I prayed that prayer and image of my wife came into my mind. It was a photograph of her when we were only married for one year. We were on our way to a friend's wedding. She was wearing a beautiful red flower dress and her hair was nicely done in a big looping curls. I can see that image vividly in my mind even now as I type this. That gave me an incredibly present sense of the Lord's healing taking place in my mind.

I have been trying to read scripture more as I go through this because I know that is essential to the renewing of my mind. As well, I have started painting again which I am taking great delight. It is a part of me that has been stifled for many years now.

Well all in all I am doing quite well. The other day I was out to the bank and I noticed my eyes starting to wander. I realized that I have only been on this new journey for just over a month and that I must remain vigilant in my quest for purity."

RECOMMENDED READING

ON PATHWAY TO GODLINESS

When Godly People Do Ungodly Things, by Beth Moore, 2002
Praying God's Word, by Beth Moore, 2000
Exiles: Living Missionally in a Post-Christian Culture, by Michael Frost, 2006

ON MEN, PORNOGRAPHY, AND ADDICTION

Pure Desire, by Ted Roberts, 1999
Sex, Men and God, by Douglas Weiss, 2002
False Intimacy: Understanding the Struggle of Sexual Addiction, by Harry W. Schaumburg, 1997
Cybersex Exposed: Simple Fantasy or Obsession, by Jennifer Schneider and Robert Weiss, 2001
Pornified: How Pornography is Transforming Our Lives, Our Relationships, and Our Families, by Pamela Paul, 2005
In the Realm of Hungry Ghosts: Close Encounters with Addiction, by Gabor Mate, 2008
The Johns: Sex for Sale and the Men Who Buy It, by Victor Malarek, 2009

ON MEN AND EMOTIONAL HEALTH

Emotionally Healthy Spirituality, by Peter Scazzero, 2006

Raising Cain: Protecting the Emotional Life of Boys, by Dan Kindlon and Michael Thompson, 2000

Let Your Life Speak: Listening to the Voice of Vocation, by Parker J. Palmer, 2000

Facing Shame: Families in Recovery, by Merle A. Fossum and Marilyn J. Mason, 1989

Self-esteem: The Cross and Christian Confidence, by Joanna McGrath and Alister McGrath, 2002

ON MARRIAGE AND PORNOGRAPHY

I Surrender All: Rebuilding a Marriage Broken by Pornography, by Clay and Renee Crosse with Mark Tabb, 2005

Living with Your Husband's Secret Wars, by Marsha Means, 1999

ON SAFEGUARDING A LEGACY OF PURITY IN THE FAMILY

False Intimacy: Understanding the Struggle of Sexual Addiction, by Harry W. Schaumburg, 1997 (Chapter 8 on Preventing Sexual Addiction in Your Children)

Pornography, by Debbie Nathan, 2007 (Chapter 10 on Censorship)

ON EXTRA-MARITAL AFFAIRS

Torn Asunder: Recovering From Extra-Marital Affairs, by Dave Carder, 1995

Torn Asunder Workbook, by Dave Carder, 2001

Safe & Sound, by Steve Hayes, 2002

The Truth about Cheating: Why Men Stray and What You Can Do to Prevent It, by M. Gary Neuman, 2008

ON WOMEN'S EXPERIENCE WITH SPOUSES' AFFAIRS AND INVOLVEMENT WITH PORNOGRAPHY

The Snare, by Lois Mowday, 1988

An Affair of the Mind, by Laurie Hall, 1996

Pure Desire, by Ted Roberts, 1999 (Two Chapters by Diane Roberts)

ON WOMEN AS KEY PLAYERS IN GOD'S KINGDOM

Women: God's Secret Weapon, by Ed Silvoso, 2001

ON WOMEN'S SEXUALITY, OBJECTIFICATION, AND SEXUAL ADDICTION

Female Chauvinist Pigs: Women and the Rise of Raunch Culture, by Ariel Levy, 2005

Black Tights: Women, Sport and Sexuality, by Laura Robinson, 2002

A History of the Breast, by Marilyn Yalom, 1997

Desire: Where Sex Meets Addiction, by Susan Cheever, 2008

ABOUT THE PURE AT HEART SEMINAR

Pure at Heart is a men's seminar on godly living in a sexualized world. It is a biblically based, teaching seminar to equip men to safeguard against pornography, sexual/emotional entanglement on the Internet, extra-marital affairs, and viewing women as sexual objects. The seminar is also designed to help men safeguard a legacy of purity in their children's lives. Since 2003, many men have attended the Pure at Heart Seminar in various Canadian cities and communities and benefited from the seminar.

Testimonials on the Pure at Heart Seminar

"I was actually turning on the computer to thank you so much for the life-changing seminar you conducted on Saturday. I have become a different person since then. To be honest I hated pornography…I knew that it was bad for my soul, mind and health. But why would I again and again reluctantly come back to it? It felt like pornography provided me something that nothing else could provide. Dr. Sheh's seminar helped me find what that "something" was and how I could obtain it in a healthy manner. He also provided me with tried and true tools to fight off pornography from my life. He showed me how to build a good defense and to

charge with a great offence, all in a warm, loving, confidential and brotherly manner. I look at women and especially my wife in a Godly way now. It is as though an elephant has been lifted off my shoulders and I can finally be productive. All of the negative energies are gone and I walk with a renewed confidence. And, best of all, my relationship with God has become more intimate because God and I fought off the enemy together. I thank God for Dr. Sheh."

"We recently had the privilege of having Dr. Simon Sheh present his 'Pure at Heart' seminar at our church. The response to Dr. Sheh's material was overwhelmingly positive. The men felt that they were provided with helpful concepts that increased their understanding of sexuality and the issues they face as men. They also felt that they had received tools which helped them to be better equipped to face the sexual temptations in our world. There was also a great appreciation for the frank and honest way in which Dr. Sheh approached the subject matter His sharing of personal stories and his own vulnerability clearly made the men feel comfortable, resulting in open interaction and the creation of an atmosphere in which men asked questions that would have been difficult to pose in almost any other setting... We hope that many more men will take advantage of this seminar in the future. We'd further like to recommend this seminar to any church interested in addressing this critical subject."

ABOUT THE
AUTHOR

Dr. Simon Sheh is a Registered Psychologist in private practice in Edmonton, Alberta, Canada. He is an approved referral counselor for Focus on the Family (Canada) Clergy Care Network and FamilyLife Canada. Dr. Sheh is the creator of Pure at Heart, a men's seminar on godly living in a sexualized world. He has a passion for sharing God's love with men and women through speaking and counseling. Dr. Sheh has appeared on the Miracle Channel and 100 Huntley Street. He has conducted seminars in Europe, Southeast Asia, and the Middle East.

For information about Dr. Simon Sheh, his Pure at Heart Seminar and speaking engagements, please contact:

Dr. Simon Sheh
www.drsimonsheh.com
simon@drsimonsheh.com
1-780-429-4761, extension 237

ACKNOWLEDGEMENTS

I gratefully acknowledge and express deep appreciation to the many wonderful people who have made this project possible:

- to Sandy Kricken, for editing the first manuscript of *Pure at Heart*
- to Mareesa Orth, for editing the final manuscript of *Pure at Heart*
- to the pastors and church leaders who brought men to the Pure at Heart seminars because they want champions of purity in the kingdom of God
- to the men who attended the Pure at Heart seminars because they want to be champions of purity in our sexualized world

BOOK ORDER INFORMATION

BY PHONE: 1-780-483-0234,
New Beginnings Bookstore,
Edmonton, Canada

BY MAIL: Complete the attached book order
form

ONLINE: Visit the *faith* section of
www.pagemasterbooks.com

IN PERSON: Inquire at your local Christian
bookstore or visit
New Beginnings Bookstore,
Buelah Alliance Church
17504 - 98a Avenue
Edmonton, Alberta 1-780-483-0234
book@beulah.ca